Women and the
Work/Family Dilemma

Women and the Work/Family Dilemma

How Today's Professional Women Are Confronting the Maternal Wall

♦ ♦ ♦

Deborah J. Swiss
Judith P. Walker

John Wiley & Sons, Inc.

New York • Chichester • Brisbane • Toronto • Singapore

Copyright © 1993 by Deborah J. Swiss and Judith P. Walker

Published by John Wiley & Sons, Inc.

Library of Congress Cataloging-in-Publication Data

Swiss, Deborah J.
    Women and the work/family dilemma : how today's professional women are confronting the maternal wall / Deborah J. Swiss, Judith P. Walker.
       p.   cm.
    Includes index.
    ISBN 0-471-53318-1 (cloth)   ISBN 0-471-03102-x (paper)
    1. Work and family—United States   2. Working mothers—United States.   3. Women in the professions—United States.   I. Walker, Judith P.   II. Title.
HD4904.25.S97   1993
331.4'4'0973—dc20   92-36038

Printed in the United States of America

10 9 8 7 6 5 4 3 2 1

To our children,

Alex and Alison Rice-Swiss

Jeff, Elizabeth, and Susan Walker

PREFACE

◆ ◆ ◆

Judy and I first met in 1980, when we were charged with developing a day-care center at the Harvard Medical School in Boston. At the time, I did not yet have children and was working for the medical school's administrative dean while completing my doctoral dissertation. Judy, whose children were in high school and college, had just been hired as the university's child care advisor.

Our first professional collaboration focused on one specific piece of the work/family puzzle. This collaboration grew, along with our friendship, as we moved through parallel life stages, but with Judy half a generation ahead of me. When I took my first maternity leave from my position as an assistant dean at the Harvard Graduate School of Design, Judy helped me find the right child care. Like many women, I returned quickly to a job that I loved, but with some regrets for too short a leave.

Judy continued her work at the university, which included advising eight hundred to nine hundred faculty, staff, and students each year on child-care issues. By the time my second child was born and I had moved to a part-time position, Judy and I began to talk regularly about the challenges and complexities of working and having a family, and about how little information is available to women on merging two important aspects of their lives.

We decided to seek funding for an in-depth survey of women who had graduated from Harvard's professional schools over a 10-year period. Initial responses to our project told us that the subject was a nonissue. Child-care options were expanding, and the increasing numbers of mothers who had entered the work force appeared to be fulfilling the super-woman myth. But our own experiences, coupled with those of the women we met in our work, convinced us that a different story about working mothers was about to break, a story that very much needed telling. With the support and enthusiasm of our agent Michael Snell, we were introduced to John Wiley & Sons, who believed a new book needed to be written for working mothers.

The stories we gleaned from 902 surveys and 52 personal interviews were even more compelling than our instincts told us they would be. This is not the book we set out to write. In the early stages of this project, we made what we thought was a safe assumption: If we surveyed a large population of women with top-flight professional credentials, we would discover many examples of support in the workplace for women confronting the career/family dilemma. But a different, nearly opposite, picture began to emerge. The vast majority of the women whom we heard from achieved their individual resolution for balance entirely on their own, with virtually no recognition in the workplace of their role as parents.

Our revised agenda became to define in honest and realistic terms how working mothers are leading their lives today. *Women and the Work/Family Dilemma* describes the powerful presence of what we term *the maternal wall*—an unfortunate accomplice to the glass ceiling. Over and over, we heard confirmation that the glass ceiling, which limits how far a woman can advance, is still firmly in place. And it is buttressed by the often transparent, yet still formidable maternal wall, which further hinders a mother's career progress.

For the past decade, women have managed away logistical conflicts between work and family, or have simply assumed all the blame when collisions occur between career demands and children's needs. A woman's choice at work has been to play the game, or challenge the rules and risk suffering a career penalty.

Without question, women have proven that they are as capable and talented in their professions as the men who sit next to them in the office. However, neither society nor our standard work ethic has in any way addressed the new demographics of the office and the home. The traditional expectations of father as breadwinner and mother as nurturer do not hold up when both parents are in the work force, and when many women must go it alone as single parents.

As surveys were returned and we began the personal interviews, we were at first discouraged by how little progress has been made, and at times shocked by what we were told. We learned that women with proven dedication to their professions find their commitment questioned by bosses and co-workers as soon as they decide to become mothers. Despite obstacles placed in their career paths by those who believe that career ambition must relegate family to a secondary priority, today's professional women have begun to forge a new identity for what it means to be a working mother.

Our research evolved into a book about life choices and about how our culture of work impacts our options: How family influences career paths and how careers affect choices about family life; what goes into making decisions about merging two important, if seemingly contradictory, roles; what advice the women we met would pass on to other women currently making decisions about balancing a professional and personal life. Finally, our research has led us to propose some new definitions for "having it all."

We hope that mothers will share this book with sons and daughters about to embark on their own careers; that husbands will read it with their wives, as they discover in their own households how to manage their dual careers; and that progressive employers will consider some of the strategies we propose for recognizing the new demographics in the work force. And we want mothers to know that they are not alone in the dilemma they face in the career/family/marriage triad. Despite certain inherent tradeoffs between work and family, we hold the optimism that the workplace *can* change in ways that will support a more comfortable alliance between careers and children.

DEBORAH J. SWISS

Lexington, Massachusetts

ACKNOWLEDGMENTS

♦ ♦ ♦

From both:

We are very fortunate to have friends who provided support and constructive criticism for every stage of this project: Marvin Green, Kathy Puccia, Roger Stix, Audrey Theodore, and Barry Walker. We truly appreciate all the support, expertise, and patience we received from our editor John Mahaney. Sydney Rozen and Martha Urban provided superb editorial skills. And, a special thank-you to our agent Michael Snell for believing in us from the start and for his consistent enthusiasm and sound advice.

For technical assistance with the project, we thank Christine Bodger, Erin Phelps, and Carl Phillips. Nora Nercessian and Simone Reagor provided invaluable help with the survey. And to the busy women who responded to our survey, we could not have written this book without your openness and support, and for that we thank you.

From Deborah:

With loving thanks to my parents, Ed and Peg Swiss, who have always encouraged me and who in so many thoughtful ways helped me finish this book. This book is dedicated with love and appreciation to my children, Alex and Alison Rice-Swiss, whose constant support and cheerful talk of bringing the book to show-and-tell kept me going and helped me to write a better book.

From Judy:

With appreciation to my mother, Jean Poley, whose caring guidance and personal strength have always inspired me. With thanks to my adult children Jeff, Elizabeth, and Susan Walker for their ongoing encouragement, assistance, and patience throughout the completion of this project. This book is dedicated to them with love.

CONTENTS

◆ ◆ ◆

Women and the
Work/Family Dilemma

INTRODUCTION

◆ ◆ ◆

The Many Dimensions of "Having It All"

For the generation that grew up during the feminist revolution and the rapid social change of the 1960s and 1970s, it at first seemed achievement enough just to "make it" in a man's world. But coupled with their ambition, today's women have developed a fierce determination to find new options for being both parent and professional without sacrificing too much to either role or burning themselves out beyond redemption.

Women have done all of the accommodating in terms of time, energy, and personal sacrifice that is humanly possible, and still they have not reached true integration in the workplace. For a complicated set of reasons—many beyond their control—they feel conflict between their careers and their children. All but a rare few quickly dispel the myth that superwoman ever existed.

For many women, profession and family are pitted against one another on a high-stakes collision course. Women's values are stacked against the traditions of their professions. In the home, men and women struggle to figure out how dual-career marriages should work. Role conflict for women reaches far beyond the fundamental work/family dilemma to encompass a whole constellation of fiercely competing priorities. Women today find themselves in an intense battle with a society that cannot let go of a narrowly defined work ethic that is supported by a family structure that has not existed for decades. The unspoken assumption persists that there is still a woman at home to raise the children and manage the household. But the economic reality is that most people, whether in two-parent or single-parent families, need to work throughout their adult lives. As a consequence, the majority of today's mothers are in the labor market.

The first full-fledged generation of women in the professions did not talk about their overbooked agenda or the toll it took on them and their families. They knew that their position in the office was shaky at best. With virtually no choice in the matter, they bought into the traditional notion of success in the workplace—usually attained at the high cost of giving up an involved family life. If they suffered self-doubt or frustration about how hollow professional success felt without complementary rewards from the home, they blamed themselves— either for expecting too much or for doing too little. And they asked themselves questions that held no easy answers: Am I expecting too much? Is it me? Am I alone in this dilemma? Do other women truly have it all?

Until now, this has been a private dilemma, unshared, as each woman was left to forge her own unique solution to merging her dual loyalties to work and family. Too often she felt that she alone had failed to achieve a comfortable balance between the two.

STRIKING THE RIGHT BALANCE

Women bristle at the notion of a "mommy track"—even if they choose to slow their careers or reduce their hours—because it is founded on assumptions determined solely by gender and labeled to define only one aspect of a woman's complex identity. Moreover, the assumptions are dangerous because any kind of tracking assumes uniformity among the group. No such uniformity exists. First, there is no one right way for a mother to lead her life. Second, people's priorities cannot remain fixed over time. At different phases of their lives, women recalibrate the balance between profession and children as careers evolve and family circumstances change.

Like men, women derive personal reward and satisfaction from achievement in their careers. Where women differ from many men is in the expectations they hold for balance in their lives. Realistic about how much one person can accomplish in a given day, women expect to have to make some trade-offs between work and family. Families, however, have absorbed all the stress and strain they possibly can. The entire responsibility for accommodation is taking place on the home side of the equation.

As things stand today for working mothers, professional ambition is pitted against maternal pride under a seemingly no-win set of rules. Working mothers hire baby-sitters to cover the home front when important clients must be entertained for dinner, yet these same mothers feel guilty when they leave work early to attend a piano recital or championship game. Briefcases can come into the home every night, but it is the rare parent who feels comfortable bringing a child to work on a school snow day. The intractable work culture often translates the work/family dilemma into an either-or choice, with little room for reasonable accommodation between the two.

Women's gender does not render them any less able than men to excel in their chosen profession. They can do their jobs as well as any man. But no one can be expected to do the impossible: to be an involved parent with little or no recognition in the workplace that they have another life outside the office.

The term *working father* is not even in our vocabulary. Society's traditional expectations exert no pressure on fathers to star as both parent and professional. And the term *working mother* is itself a misnomer because all mothers "work" long hours even if not at a paid job.

As long as a woman plays by the male rules of the game, the career doors stay open. Proving she can do her job is not enough. As soon as she proposes a different agenda for combining a career with an involved family life, doors in the professions begin to swing shut. Despite the rapid evolution and expansion in women's roles in the last decade, the roles of men at home and the rules for success in the office have barely moved. Reflected in deeply entrenched attitudes about how to be a "professional," and intensified by the realities of who does what in the home, today's rules of work dictate that one critical aspect of a woman's life is destined to be out of balance.

Because there is so little real support for parenting issues in the workplace, women view the high potential for collision between their careers and their children as a unique personal problem. No one—man or woman—can have it all without support from the workplace and genuine help at home. Women, regardless of how they have chosen to lead their lives, can now breathe a collective sigh of relief that superwoman is dead. Women are not alone in the self-doubt and ambivalence they face in their individual struggle to locate the right balance between two important aspects of their lives.

GETTING THE TRUE PICTURE

We set out to discover how women in the professions are confronting their complex agendas of career, children, spouses, and personal life satisfaction. We thought that if we surveyed some of the "best and brightest" we would learn how they have achieved balance through creative approaches to the work/family question. If anyone would have the answers, women from Harvard's Business, Law, and Medical schools would seem to be likely candidates. We assumed that the women we surveyed had it all. What we found is not what we expected.

Women in the professions are *doing* it all. They have proven to themselves—and even to their harshest critics—that women *can* manage both a career and a family. Yet for many, the personal toll is not worth the price. Clearly ambitious and with top-notch professional credentials, these well-trained and dedicated women nevertheless told us that no one has it all, even if from all outward appearances they appear to do it all.

Many of the women we met have merged their dual roles successfully and avoided a major collision between their often competing worlds, but none has escaped without trade-offs and personal sacrifice, or struggle and inner conflict. Dedicated to their professions and committed to their children, these women reveal the fragile and tenuous line they walk as they attempt to manage a career on one side and a family on the other. What they told us is both shocking and provocative.

Again and again the stories shared by women across the country revealed a work culture dominated by ''Old Boys'' who have imposed a glass ceiling to limit—solely because of gender—how high women can advance in their careers. This powerful barrier is reflected in career advancement controlled by men accustomed to promoting those cast in their own mold, in exclusion from the informal and powerful Old Boy network and, ultimately, in unfair restrictions on opportunities for women to prove their abilities.

The glass ceiling has remarkably few cracks despite an impressive generation of women armed with credentials equal to any man's. And, we discovered, the glass ceiling is firmly buttressed by a maternal wall—a transparent but very real barrier that significantly hinders a mother's ability to balance successfully work and family.

Together these formidable, yet often camouflaged barriers place women in double jeopardy. Based on the current rate at which women are being promoted, and assuming that the pace of change for women does not accelerate, this painfully slow process will take 475 more years before women achieve full and equal participation in the executive suites.[1]

Many women first encounter the maternal wall when they

announce a pregnancy. Bosses and co-workers begin to question the woman's professional commitment and ability to sustain her high productivity and performance. The maternal wall is securely in place when:

- A male mentor, whose own wife stayed at home to raise their children, tells his protege, "Take my advice. Don't take your whole maternity leave. Not if you want to keep your job."

- A woman is told by her supervisor, "We filled your position. Call me when you're not pregnant anymore."

- A request from a top performer to job share in order to spend more time with her new baby brings this instant response from her boss, "It can't happen. It's never been done."

- Clients are reassigned to others, without cause or warning, solely because a woman announces a pregnancy.

We intentionally chose to study a group of women in the professions whose background and training would be highly competitive with any sample of men in the same fields. We wanted to know to what extent gender—in and of itself—affects the work/family dilemma. We found that even top-flight professional credentials do not indemnify a woman from the damaging barriers imposed by the maternal wall. Moreover, women who wait to have children until their careers are well-established may be no more immune from the penalties imposed by the maternal wall than are younger women with less well-established careers. The biases imposed by the maternal wall follow women all the way up the corporate ladder.

In 1960, 19 percent of mothers with children under age six worked outside the home. By 1990, that number had skyrocketed to 56 percent; and, for women with children aged 6 to 17,

73 percent were in the work force.[2] Women now constitute half of the population entering the professions of business and law and 40 percent of those entering the field of medicine.

By the year 2000, two-thirds of the new entrants into the work force will be women, and 75 percent of these women will bear at least one child during their working years.[3] The workplace and the values of society that support the prevailing work ethic have barely begun to recognize that life in the office needs to reflect the radical changes that have occurred in the home.

The treatment of working mothers in the mass media mirrors this culture's ambivalence and confusion about women's contemporary roles, and reflects society's inability to offer new solutions to the work/family dilemma. Media attention on working mothers ranges from the contradictory—"Babies Need Their Mothers at Home" versus "Why It Pays to Keep on Working"—to downright inflammatory—"Mommy vs. Mommy." Only one theme unifies this emotionally charged topic: balancing work and family persists as one of the major unresolved issues in American life.

Headlines like "Protecting Your Powerbase When You're on Maternity Leave," "Fighting to Have It All," "Will You Be Penalized for Having a Baby?" "Mothers Who Take Extended Time Off Find Their Careers Pay a Heavy Price" fuel a woman's anxiety by warning that, regardless of the choice she makes, some important piece of her life will suffer. To intensify this dilemma, it is only the women—not their husbands—who are made to feel they must struggle with the ultimate choice: career *or* child.

A fall 1990 special issue of *Time* devoted exclusively to women's issues expressed a sentiment that could easily chill the heart of any working mother: "The Great Experiment: Today's parents are raising children in ways that little resemble their own youth. The question that haunts them: Will the kids be all right?"[4]

The Survey

Women and the Work/Family Dilemma reveals the life choices, conflicts, and advice of the 902 women who responded to our survey and includes the comments of 52 women who agreed to an in-depth personal interview. The work/family dilemma clearly hits a sensitive nerve among this generation of working women. A mailing of 1,644 surveys yielded 902 responses, an extraordinarily high response rate of 55 percent. The first response, from a mother of two, was completed and returned in just four days. The last came in 1½ years later from a single woman who had been held as an involuntary "guest" of the government of Saudi Arabia.

Who are the women we heard from? Of the 902 Harvard women who responded, 341 are graduates of the Business School, 332 are from the Law School, and 229 are from the Medical School. Eighty-nine percent of the women are currently in the work force. Purposely we surveyed women who, as "delayed childbearers," would be in the midst of their childbearing years.

Three-quarters of the group are married. Two-thirds are mothers, and most have children 12 years of age and under. Twenty-eight percent have one child; 52 percent have two children, and the rest have three or more. Two women, remarried and with stepchildren, reported seven children in their families. The predominant age range of the women is from 33 to 45. Of those who do not have children, 40 percent say that they plan to have children in the future.

The Findings

The women's individual stories describe a wide range of options for how to resolve the conflict between careers and children, and include:

- The pros and cons of a part-time job.

- Who decides to become an entrepreneur and what propels them to strike out on their own.

- Why so many professionally trained career women are opting to be at home full-time with their children.

- How women have carved out satisfying careers and supportive partnerships in the home.

- What forces some women out of their profession.

- The points of collision between work and family, and what can be done to try to avoid them.

- Strategies for avoiding the maternal wall and ways to regroup if you hit it.

- The essential components in both the office and the home for women who want to achieve success as mothers and professionals.

A few extraordinary individuals navigate with ease the intensely turbulent waters that swirl around them and compete so fiercely for their time and energy. Others have a few close calls but manage to stay afloat. Some women experience a painful collision between their motivation to excel in the workplace and the emotional tug to be with their children. Some of these strike out on their own and get back on track with their own unique game plans for developing a rewarding career along with time to enjoy a family. Another option is to sequence career and family, staying home for a period of time and then returning to the workplace. Some women find that their best option is simply to change to a job in a more ''parent friendly'' work culture.

Some of the women we met have managed to avoid both the glass ceiling and the maternal wall. Others told us what happened when they felt they had lost control of their lives and relinquished their personal definition of success. They also revealed how they put the pieces back together—this time according to their own rules and not those dictated by the traditions of their professions. Individually, they have begun to develop more comfortable ways to converge their many roles.

The complicated roles of working women are still in the midst of rapid evolution and challenge. As the women we met spoke honestly about their conflicts, successes, and defeats in striking a balance between their careers and their children, we quickly learned that today's woman is not as far along as we thought. This book describes what working women face as they attempt to forge new definitions for getting the best from two important aspects of their lives.

The 902 women surveyed revealed that:

- Eight-five percent believe that reducing hours of work is detrimental to a woman's career. Despite this widely held perception, 70 percent of the mothers decreased their hours after the birth of their first child.

- Of the 594 mothers, 53 percent have changed their jobs or specialty because of family responsibilities.

- Ninety-six percent of the mothers returned to work before their first child was a year old, with 82 percent taking a maternity leave of four months or less.

- The dropout rate for the mothers in business is extraordinarily high. Twenty-five percent of the respondents who have a Masters of Business Administration (MBA) degree from Harvard have left the workplace entirely, many feeling that they had been forced out of the best jobs once they became mothers.

- Even though we did not ask a question about fertility

problems, 230 of the 902 told us that fertility has been a problem for them.

- While 39 percent of the mothers believed that having children slowed their careers, 85 percent said that they have been able to combine career and family successfully, even if everything has not gone according to their original plan.

We quickly learned that no one had ever asked these women about their lives and their individual struggle to merge work and family. Once we did, the floodgates opened. We have all seen the public professional side of these women. In corporations, law firms, and hospitals, they appear to do their jobs with ease and efficiency. And they do. But we got to know them from another perspective. They allowed us to see the private side of the equation. We saw the whole woman: mother, professional, and wife. *Women and the Work/Family Dilemma* presents a snapshot of the lives of working mothers.

Women expressed anger and frustration that expectations and reality were so far apart. One MBA, now at home, explained her disappointment: "With the women's movement, there was this promise held out that you could do everything. And for a long time I grappled with that and felt ripped off and angry. From the outside, and only from the outside, I did have it all."

One by one, their individual stories unfolded to reveal some sad, yet all-too-common themes: mothers afraid to take maternity leaves for fear of long-term economic repercussions; women who delivered babies on Friday and returned to work on Monday, having been informed by male colleagues that these are the rules of the game; talented women forced out of a workplace that dictates 70-hour weeks or nothing. Fear of reprisal on the job was the primary reason some of the women surveyed requested use of a pseudonym.

As highly trained professionals, these women readily admit

that they have been fortunate in their education, career opportunities, and earning potential. Yet even women with the most solid credentials and the financial ability to arrange the best possible child care are finding it difficult to merge their dual roles.

The desire to find time for family life crosses all economic groups and is a unifying theme for this generation of working women at all levels of the workplace. No one solution to the work/family merger will work for every woman, but working mothers who read this book should come away with some new strategies for attaining a more peaceful alliance between profession and family. They should also find comfort in knowing that they are not alone in their individual struggle.

Conclusions

Certain key themes emerge from this study of working mothers:

- They are looking for answers.

- Quick and painless solutions don't exist.

- The unresolved issues will require fundamental change in the workplace and in the home.

- As much as they want to be part of the solution for solving the work/family dilemma, women are not the problem.

Women are angry and frustrated. And for good reason. A collective wave of anger is beginning to generate a new movement among women, a movement to force society to confront and deal with the unnecessary conflict between careers and children. In spite of the heavy odds stacked against them, they refuse to contemplate that their children—and their daughters in particular—will have to face the same rough water that they have been forced to navigate in their competing roles of mother and professional.

At long last, women feel that the time is right to speak with their true voice. Today's generation expects more: a new definition of success that includes the home front as well as the work world. What is different about this postfeminist generation is that women are speaking up to say, "It's not easy to be a working mother in today's world. I don't want to be like the men and deny that the unyielding rules of my profession conflict with my desire for a good, sane, family life." Without support for women—at home and at work—careers and children *are* destined to be on a collision course. Until now, the entire burden for figuring out how to do it all has fallen solidly on the woman.

The potential for achieving better balance is there, but the vast majority of businesses have failed to advance and support solutions for a more comfortable alliance between profession and family. Even in organizations that offer parental benefits, the policies on paper are often a distant reality from what is allowed in practice for women who want to keep their careers on track.

A Philadelphia pediatrician and mother of three, in answer to a query about support in her work environment, responded, *"What support!?!?!"* Then she added, "We actually fail to support ourselves by failing to take what we need for our families. My colleague took two weeks off after her second child was born—and that became the standard."

Is it possible to have a challenging job *and* a reasonable workweek? What type of accommodation for parents constitutes exploitation for the employer? At what point does an employer risk losing its most promising talent?

What works for one woman will not necessarily work for another. Women need to feel that they will not be ostracized by society, by their profession, or even by other mothers for making the choice that is most comfortable for them. For one woman at this point in her life, the choice may be to stay home. For another, the solution to her grueling 70-hour workweek is to hire live-in help to support her at home and to cover all contingencies. Some women slow their career while their children are young. For others, the answer is self-employment, while still others have discovered that they can sustain a career while working part-time.

In the 1960s, Betty Friedan ignited a movement that would forever change how women perceive the happy homemaker. In *The Second Stage*, Friedan cautioned women not to forget about their personal lives or ignore the rewards of a family. Now professional women are on the verge of a breakthrough as they begin to mobilize and address head-on the seemingly inherent conflict between their careers and their children.

Women must first regain and then reformulate what Shirley Chisholm called "the good fight,"[5] which begins with individual, uphill struggle, gains momentum from the strength of collective voices, and forges new territory that will broaden choices for the next generation.

Betty Friedan was a pioneer in liberating and mobilizing women to deal with "the problem that has no name"[6]—the need for women to assert their independence and intelligence outside the home. The feminist movement began by determining that equality for women in the workplace meant gaining entry for women into the professions. But access to the professions is only the first battlefront. The next critical battle is to fit all of the pieces together in the work/family merger through real change in the workplace and through mobilizing women to act collectively. Then parents can make real choices in which neither family nor career will suffer.

CHAPTER ONE

◆ ◆ ◆

The Diana Penalty: Professions Against the Family

Laura Tosi, MD, has been proving herself since she was a little girl. Her father questioned the value of educating women. Her high school principal told her that she would never be admitted to medical school. Today she is one of fewer than two hundred board-certified female orthopedic surgeons in the country, and it's still a challenge to be accepted as an equal.

It is 7:00 A.M. in the nearly deserted but brightly lit Orthopedic Department of the Children's National Medical Center in Washington, D.C. Moving quickly, Dr. Tosi leads an all-male group of residents back from morning rounds. Her 80-hour week began at 4:00 A.M., when she plowed through a stack of paperwork, then fed and changed her 21-month-old son while her 5-year-old daughter slept. By 6:00 A.M. she had left the children in the care of her husband (who would wait at home for the arrival of their nanny at 7:30 A.M.) and was on her way to the hospital.

Dr. Tosi's children were both born on a Saturday and, in each case, she was back seeing patients part-time on Monday. "I felt that if I took a maternity leave, it would be viewed as proof that women don't belong in surgery. Men typically would receive extra compensation for many of the things I do," Dr. Tosi says. "The perception persists that women are not breadwinners for their families." The signals are painfully clear: a heavier work load and a lower salary than male physicians with identical credentials and work history and the same patient load.

"There is the perception in my field that, if you are a mother, you couldn't possibly be doing the job the rest of the guys are and so you shouldn't be paid as much. I am not viewed as a breadwinner for my family."

She has painstakingly followed the rules of work established by her specialty and has paid a price for this at home. To accommodate her professional training and to launch her career, she endured a commuter marriage for nine years, including three years of a grueling commute from Los Angeles to the East Coast. For one year she lived in Toronto while her husband lived in Washington, D.C.; for five years she commuted weekly from New York to Washington.

Now she and her husband, an executive in the federal government, live in the same city. Dr. Tosi recognizes his support and pride in her accomplishments, but she must also grapple with his frequent resentment for the sheer number of hours she spends at the hospital.

A recent conversation with her daughter was a painful, poignant reminder of the fundamental conflict between Laura Tosi's career and her children. Her daughter asked why she couldn't just work in a shop like her friend's mom. "What would make you say that?" Dr. Tosi asked. Her daughter answered, "So you could be at home with me."

"That really hurt," Dr. Tosi admits.

Three generations have challenged Laura Tosi's deep commitment to her profession: her father's generation who thought that women did not belong in the professions; the men in college and graduate school who believed that women were not serious about careers and only taking places away from men; and her family who resents the long hours her profession demands.

She echoes the lament of today's professional woman when she talks of how thinly she is stretched. "I have very little time to do research and to climb the academic ladder. I have given up all hobbies and rarely have time for myself."

Dr. Tosi also places high expectations on herself. "I look at myself and find my own worst enemy. I assume if I don't work harder than the men, I will be judged inferior."

Has Laura Tosi been able to combine career and family successfully? An outsider might look at her life and answer heartily, "Yes!" Certainly her economic status and her professional reputation are symbols of a version of success that few men or women will ever attain. But she herself is not so sure. "No one ever promised that combining career and family would be easy, but 'having it all' comes at a price."

WHAT IS THE DIANA PENALTY?

Like many women who have fought hard to make it to the top of their professions, Laura Tosi has had to overcome the obstacles that arise solely because of a difference in one chromosome. Her story is hauntingly reminiscent of the professional barriers encountered in 1883 by Dr. Mary Putnam Jacobi (the first woman admitted to the New York Academy of Medicine), who said, "You are liable to be so frequently reminded that you are women physicians that you can easily forget that you are, first of all, physicians."[1]

Many of the most highly motivated and comprehensively trained women in the country never anticipated that they would have to pay a price for being born female or for choosing to have children. They did not expect to feel that they would be forced to accept losses—either at work or at home—simply for wanting to achieve success in both of their worlds. For these women, whose self-image is so closely aligned to their professional identities, the price can be, at best, unsettling and, in many cases, devastating.

We call this dual conflict between career and family the

Diana Penalty. Even the most ancient portraits of ambitious women have pointed to the likelihood of failure for women who enter male territory. Like the modern woman, the complex Roman goddess Diana was born into contradictions, yet assumed her multiple roles with conviction and independence. The twin sister of Apollo, Diana forged her own strong character as the powerful goddess of the hunt. Though a huntress, she became known as a protector of nature. Though a chaste woman without children, she became the goddess of childbirth. The story of the powerful Diana is a myth laden with contradictions. Our book will attempt to untangle the contradictions faced by the modern Diana. Today's Dianas are women who fought to gain entrance into the most competitive graduate schools in the country. They are unwilling to accept failure that is based *not* on their abilities, but on their simple refusal to abide by the male rules of the game.

Laura Tosi is just one example of highly successful professional women who do not quite fit into the world they have chosen. The pattern is familiar. These women are tough. They are ambitious. They have learned to function with very little sleep and little chance for leisure. They demonstrate physical and mental stamina to rival the best of either sex. Through trial and error, they know how to deflect irritating and inappropriate comments from their mostly male peers. Far too often for it to be an accident, they are placed under unfair and unnecessary scrutiny in the workplace simply because of their gender.

These women's lives do not always meet the high expectations they have set for themselves. As they slip quietly in to kiss their children good-night, often after the children are asleep, they worry about the legacy of stress and frustration they are passing on to the next generation of women. They also suffer grave doubts about the quality of their own lives. And yet they know that in the overall scheme of things, they have been quite lucky.

THE MYTH OF "HAVING IT ALL"

When we began writing this book, we intended to present stories about success: creative examples of how the best and the brightest women in the country are forging new solutions to achieve a successful balance between work and family. However, a very different, more troubling picture has emerged from our research.

All too often, women are still being penalized for their choice to have children, no matter how well they are performing on the job. Unlike their male colleagues and husbands, many women face a seemingly no-win situation. When their jobs pit them against their family needs, these women—ambitious, driven, and dedicated to their careers—are left to wonder whether they have failed their professions, or even themselves.

Many of the MBAs, lawyers, and physicians who we surveyed said no one in graduate school or by professional example had warned them of how heart wrenching their individual choices would become. Many also admitted that they would not have listened to someone else's advice, because their own intense drive and stamina had fooled them into believing that they could "have it all."

Survey after survey pointed to unfair penalties imposed on women in the workplace:

- Obstacles to taking maternity leaves or denying themselves leave for fear of repercussions on the job.

- Serious problems with work reentry after taking a maternity leave.

- Hostile, career-derailing behavior from colleagues and bosses in response to the decision to become a mother.

- Constant uphill struggle for acceptance and equality in the still male-dominated professions.

"Having it all" is a myth. Many of the women we surveyed *have* found successful paths to resolving the work/family dilemma, but not in the ways we initially had expected. These women have achieved professional and personal balance, fulfillment, and peace of mind by recognizing and accepting that they *cannot* have it all—at least, not *all at once*. Even women who remained on the fast track after their children were born have made individual choices based on compromise and reality. They acknowledge that their choices aren't perfect, but they are far better than the alternatives: guilt, stress, and resentment at home *and* at work.

Their experiences can help other women realize that they are not alone. Their solutions can provide hope and realistic ideas for other women caught in the same trap. But first it is important to understand the political and personal roots of the Diana Penalty faced by women today.

BEYOND "THE SECOND STAGE"

In 1963 Betty Friedan's *The Feminine Mystique* set in motion a revolution whose momentum brought women into a new set of roles outside the home. Women of the postfeminist generation entered professions fully expecting the best of career and family. For 20 years, Friedan and other women's advocates had been assuring them that it was, without question, possible for them to have careers like the men. And that premise proved true.

Then in 1981 Friedan's *The Second Stage* told women that family, too, is important. But there was no history, no precedence, no sense of how rough it would be once the stay-at-home mother and working-father model disappeared. Women struggled to find answers individually because no one really knew how to merge the dual and competing roles of parent and professional.

As a group, women found themselves exhausted and conflicted. Men's roles in the family and the traditional male culture at work refused to move and evolve, whereas women were forced to choose between two crucial aspects of their lives.

Today, from outward appearances, professional women *are* making it. They represent career success stories of which the feminist movement can be proud. Yet something profoundly important is missing for them. They do their work and perform well. They care deeply about their children and families. Yet they continue to wonder what they are missing in each of their worlds.

Mothers in the work force, who may feel that they should somehow be doing better in managing their obligations at work and at home, may find ironic consolation in realizing that MBAs, physicians, and lawyers who are well-established in their careers have not yet found all the answers. They, too, have been disappointed by:

- The women's movement, which offered them the answers for only one aspect of their lives: how to have careers just like the men's.

- The rigidity of their professions demonstrated in a workplace that shows very little concern for the needs of families and children.

- Their own struggle to resolve their guilt at leaving their children while they work.

- Lack of support at home and at work, which intensifies the guilt they may feel.

The most punishing aspect of the Diana Penalty comes from within: the penalty of unrealized expectations. Even as young girls, many females question their gender role expectations. As adolescents, many of today's professional women recognized something in themselves that fiercely fought the price of being born female. Laura Tosi, for example, knew from age 12 that she *would* become a doctor. "I am such a stubborn soul. If you tell me I can't do something, I *assure you*, I will."

This is the generation that expected to do it all, the "bridge" generation that would seize the best of two worlds and carve out family roles to benefit mother, father, and children. Instead, these women are severely overburdened. Kit Wheatley, an attorney with the Federal Reserve Board, expressed the feelings of many women. "I find myself doing most of what my mother did *and* most of what my father did at home. Am I alone?"

The answer, we discovered, is no. Professional women are trying to build coherence where it has never existed, and to create new rules for managing their multiple roles. They face daily challenges in the unchartered territory they have entered. Trying to reconcile two central aspects of their lives forces them to face the toughest of all critics: themselves.

CAREER IS NOT ENOUGH

A single, 35-year-old MBA states the themes expressed by many of her classmates.

"Frankly, sometimes I think I am part of an overlooked but particularly confused generation of women: Those who grew up reading Sally, Dick, and Jane books that reflected the classic 1950s view of the family; expressed in their high school year-books their plans to be teachers, nurses, stewardesses (they were good 'till I get married' or 'go-back-to-work-after-the-kids' jobs). But we discovered somewhere in college or, as in my case, in my first job on Wall Street, that we, too, could play with the boys. And we set off to make the sacrifices and find the glory."

As she ends her six-month professional sabbatical, this former international businesswoman admits, without apology, "After 13 years of a great career and lots of fun, I find that not only am I *really* interested in having little Sallys, Dicks, and

Janes, but I am *not* very interested in leaving them with a nanny 70 hours a week." Now living in Italy and working at a slower paced job with minimal travel, she has decided to make up for all the years she put aside a personal life for the sake of her career.

When we asked investment banker Leni Darrow if she has been successful in combining career and family, she responded: "Perhaps. But it's not a fair question. Each side has to some degree fallen between the cracks." Does she believe she has paid a price professionally for being a mom? "Sure," she said, "but my kids are a zillion times more important to me than any job."

The most pervasive Diana Penalty for professional women is recognizing that their life's ambitions—broader and more complicated than most men's—may be unattainable, largely because of an unyielding work culture. They have discovered that career alone is not enough. Many want children, too.

MICRO-INEQUITIES

With topflight credentials in hand, this generation of working women was ready to make it to the top, or at least to be truly accepted as professionals by their male peers and male bosses. Many a young woman found, however, that the same signals from family and culture that had challenged her childhood ambitions did not relent, even when the little girl grew up and was graduated from Harvard Medical School.

Survey after survey pointed to the glass ceiling that still refuses to budge for professional women. And beneath the glass ceiling? Unequal pay, smaller bonuses, subjective promotion systems, verbal harassment, few willing career mentors, and direct and unnecessary challenges to a woman's role as mother.

At first these astute, accomplished MBAs, lawyers, and physicians did not want to believe that the seemingly subtle actions they encountered, first in the classroom and then in the work-place, were, in fact, forms of discrimination. Mary Rowe, a labor economist by training and an administrator at the Massa-chusetts Institute of Technology, calls these signals "micro-inequities: destructive but nonactionable aspects of the work environment that occur at the level of individual decision-mak-ing—instances in which people are treated inequitably but not in a way that can be taken to court."[2]

Micro-inequities that occur daily in the lives of professional women may, by themselves, seem inconsequential. Over time, however, they may severely constrain a woman's career prog-ress and blur her perception of her own competence. They often are hidden in the informal channels of communication within an organization; their source may be the people who have the power to make decisions.[3]

As we heard from nearly every woman we interviewed, micro-inequities multiply for the professional who also chooses to be a mother. For example, in a study conducted by Harvard Medical School, female residents reported that, when they re-turned from maternity leave, they found themselves omitted from hospital committees and from lists for conferences and departmental social events. Some recalled that, once they be-came pregnant, other physicians stopped talking informally to them in the halls or dropped them from their mentoring group.[4] What appeared, at first glance, to be short-term professional snubbing quickly translated into long-term career penalties in advancement and promotions.

In business, many MBAs have noticed that offers of plum assignments diminish with each month of pregnancy. A high-tech computer executive and member of our survey pilot group overheard her boss ask the training department staff why they were sending her to a conference "when she won't want to come back to us when her baby is born." When she did return to work after a three-week maternity leave, her boss asked, "Why aren't you going after that new job in the department?

Has your ambition gone away now that you have two children?"

In cases like this, a woman's career advancement is obviously in danger, yet she does not dare challenge decisions that are not fully public and are being made by the very people who will evaluate her performance.

Attitudes by top brass are often the source of micro-inequities, as is demonstrated by the case of Barbara Sullivan, an MBA in New York City.

A senior manager at a major bank, Barbara decided to use a direct and rational approach by discussing her maternity leave in the context of her career goals. She felt optimistic and energetic about both aspects of her life, but her boss's response was unconditional. "You will never be considered for my job if you take a maternity leave. I don't think you'll ever come back." (His own wife had quit her job when she became pregnant.)

Barbara did return to the bank after a three-month leave, but from her first day back, her boss gave both subtle and explicit messages that her time away from the bank had taken her off the advancement track.

Barbara decided to start her own business.

Bosses and colleagues often make hasty, though mistaken, assumptions about a woman's ability and determination to succeed in multiple roles, no matter how well she is performing on the job.

One investment banker discovered that her clients had been reassigned within a week after she disclosed her pregnancy. Her boss, new to his own job, was skeptical of *any* woman's ability to perform, regardless of her years of proven experience. This talented MBA suffered the unfortunate experience of hitting both the glass ceiling and the maternal wall at the same time.

As many women discover when they encounter the maternal wall, some bosses tend to forget any objective measures of performance when a woman becomes pregnant.

THE PRICE OF PREGNANCY

A vice-president of a Fortune 500 company said, "I had my first child in 1974—before many 'executive women' were having children and returning to work. I took four weeks with my first, under pressure at work and a betting pool that I would not return!" Women today continue to be pressured, tested, and labeled as "unprofessional," she observes, simply because their pregnancies demonstrate their role as mother.

We did not expect to find hostile and prejudicial behavior in the workplace directed toward well-established professionals as soon as they announced a pregnancy. The number of women in our survey who pointed to their experience with this type of discrimination alerted us to a disturbing trend.

Unsettling signs of the maternal wall emerged:

- Loss of jobs.

- Unforeseen changes in professional responsibilities.

- Roadblocks to arranging maternity leaves.

- Barriers to job reentry.

- Deteriorating work relationships.

- Resentment and, at times, outright hostility from other professionals.

Careers stagnated, self-esteem plummeted and, in some cases, a woman's health suffered. Many women reported that their visibly pregnant state seemed to make other professionals uncomfortable and brought out the worst kind of insensitive behavior from their colleagues.

Toward the end of her pregnancy, Dr. Ellen Downing* arrived at a three-hour meeting and found that all the chairs were

*An asterisk after a name designates a pseudonym.

taken. No one offered her a seat. "Not one other physician recognized that I might need to sit down." They seemed to be giving Dr. Downing a message: You're a woman. You're a doctor. You chose to be pregnant. So tough it out.

A woman's visible pregnancy is a constant reminder to her colleagues, bosses, clients, or patients that she has a personal life. During their pregnancies, many women in our survey discovered a bonding with their secretaries. The people who worked for them seemed to treat them with greater acceptance of their "humanness." At the same time, many also reported verbal harassment from male colleagues whose wives did not work outside the home and from single women who did not have children.

Many women acknowledged that their pregnancies might create legitimate concerns from peers worried that their own work loads might increase or productivity might decline during the leave of absence. However, the women were willing to make compensation for any time they were away from their jobs, and did not feel they deserved to be penalized simply because they had chosen to have a child.

One of the most unsettling stories came from Dr. Beverly Tate,* a neurologist from California. In the fall of 1985, Dr. Tate had recently launched a solo practice and was pregnant with her first daughter. Because her own patient load was light, she took a part-time job to supplement her income by working one afternoon a week in the outpatient clinic of a county hospital.

"The pay was poor, the commute was long, and the patient work load nonstop, but at least it was a reliable cash flow," she said. "And I thought I was providing a service in an area that needed it."

On top of the nausea and fatigue that she felt in early pregnancy, Dr. Tate also caught the flu and became quite ill. She decided she needed two weeks off from the clinic—the equivalent of two afternoons. She arranged for superior coverage by a neurologist well known and highly respected at the hospital.

When she approached the director of out-patient services with her plan to cover two weeks of sick leave, he fired her. "He found it unacceptable. He didn't discuss it. He just very abruptly said, 'Why don't you call me when you're not pregnant any more?' "

The director's response left Beverly Tate speechless. She was particularly disturbed because of her involvement in the care of several long-term patients. "I didn't have the opportunity to say goodbye to them or arrange for their future care. All of a sudden, I disappeared from their lives." Against her will and without her consent, Dr. Tate had become a victim.

Her anger and frustration over this incident has diminished, but not fully retreated. She is confident that she will always be a caring and dedicated physician, but this experience has jaded her view of medicine and led to a radical reassessment of her priorities for career and family. Beverly Tate is determined to make family her top priority for the rest of her life and is certain that her personal values also make her a more compassionate doctor. When anyone dares to question her ability to be both a physician and a mother, she now sets them straight without hesitation and refuses to be penalized in either of her roles.

THE LAW VERSUS THE FACTS

The spirit of the law has little clout in the workplace. The work culture, not the courts, determines how people are treated on a daily basis. The professional work ethic derived from a social structure created by men whose wives did not work outside the home. If a woman deviates from this work ethic, more often than not she finds herself forced out of the professional mainstream and off her career track.

Title VII, intended to remedy discrimination on the basis of sex, was passed as an amendment—almost as an after-thought—to the Civil Rights Act of 1964.[5] However, it does *not* protect a woman from losing her job when she becomes pregnant. It "requires companies with 15 or more employees to treat pregnancy as they would any other medical disability."[6] The history of the passage of Title VII serves as an unfortunate prophecy for how the law would unfold.

The Civil Rights Act was initially proposed as protection against racial discrimination. Wendy Kaminer points out in *A Fearful Freedom*, "The word *sex* was added to the law by a white Southern Democrat in an attempt to retard its passage or, according to some observers, as a joke."[7] Discrimination on the basis of pregnancy or childbirth is *not* a violation of constitutional rights.

"One recent analysis of employment-discrimination claims filed from 1985 through 1990, by assistant professors William Slonaker and Ann Wendt at Wright State University in Dayton, Ohio, found that new mothers were 10 times more likely to lose their jobs after taking disability leave than employees taking other kinds of medical leaves."[8]

What does protect a woman's right to employment? Why is it that equality in the workplace means something different for women? Must women pay a personal price for equality in their professions?

Even feminists cannot agree on what it means to be "equal." Feminist thought is split over the legal issues surrounding special maternity privileges for women in the workplace. One group is convinced that special dispensation will put women further behind men. Another group is certain that the biological facts of pregnancy require a different standard of benefits and some reasonable recognition of the parental demands unique to women.

Can equality include differential treatment for women who become pregnant? If a woman chooses *not* to do it all at once—if she decides to reduce her hours at work or to extend her maternity leave—must she be considered a professional failure?

If bosses and colleagues dare to discriminate against the professional, well-established women in our study, what, then, is happening to women who are in less senior positions? Pregnancy discrimination may have become more subtle but is no less widespread, and may, in fact, be on the increase, concluded a 1992 *Working Woman* special report.

> *"Charges of pregnancy discrimination filed with the EEOC [Equal Employment Opportunity Commission] actually rose 7 percent last year, to 3,023, after four straight years of decline. . . . 9 to 5, a national working women's association based in Cleveland, has fielded more than 20,000 calls about pregnancy discrimination over the past three years."*[9]

No two women have identical experiences with pregnancy or work reentry. Some women sail through both without encountering unfounded and unnecessary roadblocks to their careers. Yet even the most careful planning cannot assure that, when a woman takes on parenting, she will be treated humanely and without penalty at work. She faces the added conflict of balancing legitimate business concerns for serving her clients with her personal need to take time to bond with her young child.

THE MYTH OF CONTROL

Loss of control is not easy to accept, particularly for women accustomed to being in charge. Just as they begin to feel confident about the prospect of combining work and family, many women find their choices foreclosed by the actions of others imposing irrational decisions on their careers. These unfair judgments, which are usually beyond a woman's control, can devastate her emotional well-being, threaten her health and, in some unfortunate cases, jeopardize the health of her child. For example:

• • •

Dr. Joan Haskell,* a cardiologist, had never taken a sick day in her nearly seven years at a Maryland hospital. She was six months pregnant with her second child when her daughter was diagnosed with leukemia. Because of her track record, she did not expect to encounter what she describes as "an extreme antiwoman sentiment, especially among men my age."

"I used my accumulated vacation time to be with my ill child, but I was still required to work the holiday weekends," Dr. Haskell remembers. "My director said, 'People are getting upset because you've taken time off. You'd better get back as fast as you can.' "

"I felt I had no choice but to get back to work, because my daughter's illness had rendered us uninsurable, and I couldn't afford to risk losing my health benefits from the hospital."

• • •

One New York attorney returned to her law firm after a four-month leave and was greeted by a boss who questioned her commitment to the profession while handing her a monthly billing report highlighting a $40,000 loss in income because of her absence. Her boss had long forgotten her strong track record at the firm and could focus only on her short-term absence.

"It was quite demoralizing," she said. "As a result, I became a sole practitioner, because I felt my future had already been compromised."

31

She had relied on federal maternity and state disability laws to secure her request for a leave and, she assumed, to guarantee her return to her career. Instead, her boss had already assumed she was off the fast track while she was away.

• • •

Many women reported that bosses and colleagues were quick to decide that their relatively short absence from the work force would penalize their professional status for the long term. A physician who works for a group practice in Pennsylvania was informed that she could never become a member of the corporation because she had taken a five-month maternity leave and could never recover the income she should have brought in for those months.

• • •

One partner at a major law firm in Philadelphia completed our survey the day she returned from a three-month leave. She never entirely stopped dealing with clients, but limited her contact to telephone conferences during her first two months away. During her third month, she built in a gradual return to the office by coming in two afternoons a week.

The rules for her return to the firm were clear. "I am expected to bill down from 1,725 hours to 1,400 hours in recognition of my child's birth. How I accomplish that within the constraints of my clients' demands is up to me."

That was the good news about this lawyer's reentry. Unfortunately, becoming a mother "irreparably damaged" her relationship with a male mentor, who began to distance himself from her career as soon as she announced her pregnancy and to stop assigning the good cases he had always sent her way.

She had not really expected him to understand. "He was not a very good father to his own children and always worked 60-hour weeks throughout his career."

• • •

Kit Wheatley has come to believe that, when she decided to become a mother, several of the partners in her former law firm held her decision against her. "All these things are so subtle," she said.

She was an associate at a large firm, in the midst of a typical 60-hour-a-week case, when she became pregnant. Her doctor reminded her that he had approved of her working full-time—but, to him, full-time meant working 40 hours a week. He firmly cautioned her against working at a heavier pace.

Convinced that she needed to follow her doctor's orders, Kit had a difficult conversation with the partner in charge of her case. "I told him I wanted to go on working on the case, but explained why I had to limit my time a bit," she said. "I did feel guilty about the other lawyers who were still working late at night and on weekends, but I also knew it would be stupid for me to do this in defiance of my doctor's orders. I wanted very much to have this baby."

Kit's relationship with this male partner deteriorated from that conversation. "He at first appeared to be totally accepting of my doctor's orders, but after that he treated me differently—as though I were unfairly resting on some special status to get out of work."

• • •

Kit Wheatley's story illustrates the effect of the work ethic on pregnant working women who encounter physical limitations to the number of hours they are able to spend on their jobs. Some women work their regular pace right up to the delivery of a child, with no negative impact on either mother or baby. Others, however, feel compelled to work a breakneck overtime pace because they fear for their job security and the possible loss of professional respect. The majority of women in our survey reported that their maternity leaves were too short.

The Diana Penalty grows steeper each time the media persist in capitalizing on the superwoman image, to the personal detriment of the "superwoman" herself. A 1990 article in *The New England Journal of Medicine* received widespread coverage for its pronouncement that women can work 100 hours per week in a high-stress field, such as medicine, and still deliver healthy babies. Once again, women were encouraged to feel guilty if they limit their weekly working hours to 50 or 60—let alone 40—during their final months of pregnancy or, heaven forbid, if they take time off for pregnancy-related complications.[10]

Like their male counterparts, most professional women set very high standards for themselves and their careers. Yet bosses and colleagues may begin to question their commitment to their jobs as soon as they announce a pregnancy—even if they have no intention of slowing down.

When Marilyn Bates,* a Washington, D.C., attorney, went public with her pregnancy, her large law firm stopped assigning her cases. "As soon as people knew I was pregnant, even though they *knew* I would be there another six months, they seemed to have the attitude that I was going to be gone at any moment. It wasn't too long before I just didn't have enough work to do."

The head of litigation stopped assigning Marilyn casework and switched her to research projects, the jobs at the bottom of the totem pole that are typically assigned to less experienced associates.

During her second pregnancy, Marilyn was working at another large law firm. Her boss, like Barbara Sullivan's, mistakenly assumed that Marilyn would not return to her profession. On one count, he was right. Marilyn chose not to work for him any longer. Seven months after her second child was born, she began a new job in a firm that evaluated her skills on her professional abilities, not on her status as "mother."

Marilyn does not yet feel completely comfortable with the choices she has made to combine profession and family. Despite her background at Wellesley College and Harvard Law School, and her current position at a government agency, she worries that she may have permanently derailed her career because she does not want to work more than 50 or 60 hours a week.

WHEN TO FIGHT BACK

Even women with topflight professional credentials feel frustrated when others make mistaken assumptions about them and their professional options. Unless a woman is willing to take the risks that come with fighting back, her career and her self-esteem can be devastated if she lets others define her work ethic. For example, although Marilyn Bates' clients tell her she is a good lawyer, she feels that the insulting job assignments she was given during each of her pregnancies undermined the personal commitment she had made to the practice of law.

Somewhat reluctantly, Marilyn Bates advises young women who are beginning to make decisions about balancing work and family life: "The law is among the worst professions for balance. Even medicine is better. Actually, law is a terrible profession for anyone with any outside interests, whether male or female."

Dr. Andrea Franklin* might disagree. An obstetrician at a hospital in California, she was asked to be the assistant chief of her department—but the job offer was withdrawn when she announced she was pregnant.

A year later, when the person given the job did not work out, Dr. Franklin was offered the position again and accepted. "Usually, when I feel discriminated against, I holler. In this case, I could have made a big stink, but I made an informed choice not to."

Colleagues often send women direct and unpleasant signals about their decision to become parents. For example, a lawyer, the mother of two, suggested that even to dare to have a baby is detrimental to a woman's career. A doctor in our survey had such difficulty arranging coverage for her maternity leave last year that, at 37, she has postponed having a second child for fear of losing her job.

Handling Reentry Problems

Reentry can be complicated because even the most careful planning cannot determine when babies choose to be born.

For Dr. Ellen Downing, a clinical researcher, four weeks' maternity leave meant leaving her premature twins who were still on a monitor and barely off tube feeding. Ellen believed at the time that she had no other options because she had heard her boss complaining about the inconvenience of other women's maternity leaves.

When she returned from her leave, Dr. Downing told her boss about her sons' condition, adding that she had been with them around the clock for the past month, with only an occasional hour of sleep.

His response? "If you're tired, I'll put a couch in your office."

Dr. Downing says she regrets that she was not more assertive about taking more time off to attend to the pressing needs of her preemies. "Oh, I was very foolish. I was just plain too tired to think straight. What I should have done was to take a leave without pay."

Discrimination often hits people precisely at their weakest point of defense. This is particularly true when new mothers return to work—and are least able to fight back. Added responsibilities at home, adjustments to new roles for both parents, and the normal fatigue that comes with caring for young children can sharpen the tension for women who are trying to balance their worlds.

For the first time a woman may begin to question her ability, and even her desire, to succeed in multiple roles. It's not that she has given up her professional ambition; rather, the hurdles she faces because she is female don't seem worthy of more personal sacrifice when the maternal tug is at its peak.

Women know that they face possible career derailment when they are absent from work for family reasons. They realize that there are legitimate instances when their absence requires immediate and full-time replacement coverage. Any absence, for whatever reason, that is greater than a few weeks may require special arrangements. Discrimination solely on the basis of a pregnancy, however, is another matter. A leave from a job should not result in a downward spiral for a woman's career.

Catalyst for Change

Some women are getting angry—or creative—enough to use a negative work culture as the catalyst for a new career opportunity. These women are fighting back. Whether they win their battle against the Diana Penalty hinges, to some extent, on luck and timing.

• • •

Joyce Fensterstock, a Wall Street fast-tracker with three children, returned from one of her maternity leaves to discover that her position had been filled by a man close to retirement.

She used the shock to her advantage, however. Her proven track record gave her a choice of several promising career paths that she might not have otherwise considered. Joyce is currently the president of mutual funds at PaineWebber.

• • •

An attorney from a large metropolitan area came back from her four-month leave, ready and eager for new assignments. But three weeks into her return to the job she had held for four years, she decided to give her notice. Why? Her supervisor criticized her harshly for going home at 5:00 P.M. to nurse her baby.

She was immediately offered, and quickly accepted, a new position. This company recognized that her need to leave early—always with a full briefcase—was a minor, short-term accommodation for a talented and loyal professional.

• • •

Of course, not all reentry problems can be solved so smoothly and with so little interruption to a woman's career. Reentry can be a particularly difficult challenge for self-employed women. Their financial stability may depend on how well and how quickly they manage their return to work.

• • •

Dr. Beverly Tate, who had her first child shortly after establishing her practice, already knew how to prepare for rebuilding a patient base. She readily admits, "It was slow starting each time. In a way, I feel as though I've started private practice three times in five years."

• • •

One MBA market development manager felt tested by the pressure to make a clear choice between work and family when her company offered her a promotion— at the cost of an early return from her maternity leave.

She refused the promotion and later chose to move to a part-time staff marketing position. She ultimately left the work force by choice, at her own pace, and under her own terms, to become a full-time mother.

WHERE DO THEY FIT?

Many women are surprised by the intensity of their maternal pulls and the conflict it brings to their competing roles. This is the precise point at which many women feel the stress of the work/family dilemma most keenly. They realize that they may have to pay a price for wanting to be both professionals and mothers. They feel guilty for not being at work, and angry for being manipulated into feeling this guilt. Usually they are physically exhausted. They don't quite fit at home. They don't quite fit at work. Where do they belong?

Fewer than one-third of the Harvard women reported that their careers had influenced their decision to have children. Most had made the choice to become a mother with confidence and optimism. The hard reality began when their dual roles refused to merge as they had planned. MBA Leni Darrow returned to 60-hour workweeks after the six-week maternity leaves she took for each of her two children, yet she feels the presence of the maternal wall. She now tells her younger colleagues, "If you want a personal life (marriage, children), don't sacrifice for work because you can give it all up for your career and there's still a very good chance you'll be a second-class citizen in the office. But you won't even realize it until it's too late."

A law partner, who put in 350 billable hours during her three-month maternity "leave" and generated millions of dollars worth of new business, believes that her male partners will always hold her temporary absence against her. She now counsels other women, "Do not defer your personal life. Men don't—and you shouldn't. You will be discriminated against as a woman whether or not you have a personal life. So don't hurt yourself by deferring happiness."

Role Overload

What happens to professional women when careers and children are not a perfect fit? Signs of role overload appear:

- Guilt.

- Stress.

- Fatigue.

- Questions about competence.

- Professional burnout.

Guilt can strike working mothers at work and at home: Guilt for leaving the office early to attend a soccer game. Regret for delegating the care of a sick child to someone the child barely knows. Worrying at work about the children's day. Worrying at home about unfinished work at the office while trying to create "quality time" with her children.

In neither role do women have a sense of "a job well done." Their frustration builds as they realize that their husbands—

as fathers and professionals—suffer no such conflict and few challenges to the roles they have chosen. An article, refuting an insulting premise about women, entitled "Child's Diet Not Compromised by Career Mother," made its way across the Associated Press wires in 1992 and read:

> " 'In spite of popular opinion that mothers' employment might be detrimental to children's diets, that was not the case in this fairly large national sample,' said lead author Rachel K. Johnson, an assistant nutrition professor at the University of Vermont at Burlington." [11]

THE BIOLOGICAL PENALTY

Some professional women may unknowingly impose on themselves the cruelest penalty of all. By deciding to delay childbearing, they may discover later that they have lost their option for motherhood.

They are finally ready to have a child. They have already proven themselves professionally. They are secure financially. They have read and felt reassured by the current research that demonstrates that women can bear healthy babies into their forties. The sad reality is that, the older a woman is, the more difficult it may be to conceive. One bank vice-president offered this advice: "Don't put off having a family too long. There is no time to catch up later. I am trying to have a child at age 40 and it is probably more distracting to my job than if I had children to take care of. And it's more difficult to have one now."

As their careers gain momentum and professional opportunities widen, these women put their personal lives on hold to give their ambition time and room to thrive. For some, however, the penalties for waiting are failed or childless marriages, or the simple lack of time to find a mate. And frustration is

41

heightened by the reality that their male colleagues have virtually no restrictions, either biological or professional, on when to have children.

AVOIDING THE PENALTY

It may not always be possible to avoid the penalties brought on by the business world's response to motherhood, but there are strategies that can reduce the risk of being penalized. MBA Sue Glasspiegel suggests, "Choose your company and mentors carefully, and ask about women's experiences with combining two lives."

Renee Matalon, a part-time Washington, D.C., attorney at a government agency, was feeling particularly feisty when she applied for her job. She asked everyone who interviewed her about their own lives outside the agency.

Renee knew she would need a supportive climate for both sides of her life, so she came right out and asked her potential boss questions that would help her decide whether to take the job. "What do you do when you're not in the office? How do you and the other people who work here use your leisure time? What kind of hours do people spend at their desks?"

The answers gave Renee a sense of the values and priorities of the people with whom she would be working, and helped her decide how those people might treat her if she became pregnant. Her instincts proved correct. She is still enjoying a rewarding career, working a four-day week.

"I have encountered absolutely no obstacles in taking maternity leave, reducing my work schedule, or refusing to travel."

Although Renee Matalon's work situation is unfortunately not typical of women's experiences with part-time professional work, her story is a fine example of how well a reduced schedule can work.

Some women in our survey also found a useful strategy in some reentry advice from child development expert T. Berry

Brazelton. He now supports mothers who work, but cautions that a mother must convey confidence about her choice to return to work, or even the youngest child may question her decision.[12] Many women have used this strategy with their bosses as well. MBA Lisa Churchville says, "People read your level of self-confidence. The more secure you are in your life decisions, the more comfortable everyone is with whatever you do."

Ann Fudge, now director of marketing and business development at Kraft General Foods, remembers with great clarity her first day of work as a newly minted Harvard MBA at another company. She received a call from her son's school, informing her that he had been seriously injured in a playground accident. Ann was doubly concerned because her son has hemophilia.

When she explained to her boss why she needed to leave, he responded, "Is this a trend? Are you going to be gone a lot?"

Ann answered, with her usual calm demeanor, "Of course, I'll do whatever I need to do for my child. If my work should suffer, tell me. But don't comment on my family unless there is a problem with my work." Since that first test early in her career, Ann established family as her first priority.

An unmarried Boston law partner offered this advice: "Have your children at one job and your career at another." Her implicit message is, hide your maternal side if you want to succeed. As discouraging as this concept may be, many professional women report that they are never treated quite the same after they become mothers. Their superiors often pit Profession against Family, with all the rules slanted so that Profession has to "win," regardless of the cost to the individual.

REALISTIC STRATEGIES

On one level, the integration of today's working mother into the workplace has been monumental. Consider the sheer number of women in professions that traditionally excluded them. To many ambitious women, however, the Diana Penalty continues to cause frustration and disappointment.

Many professional women are still being made to pay for their choice to become mothers, even if they also choose to maintain their high degree of dedication to their careers. They are left to wonder if they alone are responsible for failing to find a comfortable way to balance their commitment to their careers and their love for their children.

Some women, however, have learned to fight back and to turn around even the most miserable and hostile situations.

Lisa Churchville, an MBA account executive, was nearly forced out of a rewarding career because of one difficult and unreasonable manager.

Lisa had done everything right in arranging a 13-week maternity leave, including full coverage by a competent and supportive group of peers. Even her clients voiced their support for her leave and looked forward to her return.

Three weeks after her baby was born, Lisa learned that she had a new boss. He called her at home with "veiled threats" about her job security and questions about her commitment to her job. He even had the nerve to ask if she knew how to arrange for child care. Lisa gave in to his verbal harassment and cut short her leave after nine weeks.

Within weeks after her return, she sat down with her new boss for her annual review. Long before the media coined the phrase, her manager informed her that she would be "mommy tracked," with reassignment of some of her major clients to others.

"He was talking about semiretirement at age 33—making me a worker-bee drone who would take on poorer accounts. He made it clear that I wasn't a player anymore because I had a child."

For a moment Lisa worried about her skills and competence. Then she reached a simple conclusion. "This is not slavery. I can leave. I really am good at this."

She considered legal action for discrimination, but knew that her company's unwritten performance review system would make her case difficult to prove and would certainly render her work environment unbearable.

Within six months, Lisa had carefully researched the work culture at competing firms and learned that a rival company was promoting impressive numbers of women and minorities. She also discovered that the company's promotion system was based on merit and ability, rather than on unwritten and highly subjective standards.

Lisa Churchville landed on her feet and actually felt liberated by her decision to leave. On her first day at the new job Lisa met other working mothers in fast-track positions and realized that she had placed herself back into a career with a future.

During the most joyous period of their lives, many professional women are made to feel that they are somehow letting down the male team by choosing to bear a child. After a while, they refuse to accept the team rules that make no sense to them and that have traditionally curtailed the range of choices for men in the work/family merger.

It may not be possible to fully dedicate yourself simultaneously to career and family with no trade-offs whatsoever. Few men have ever done so. Many of the women we surveyed offered these suggestions as realistic strategies to blunt or avoid the Diana Penalty:

- **Start your family when your career is strong.** Never enter a maternity leave on shaky professional ground.

- **Be realistic about how your life will change after the birth of your child.** Be prepared for the possibility that even your most careful plans cannot anticipate every conflict between career and children.

- **Negotiate professional flexibility from a position of strength.** Provide your boss and partners with a detailed plan for how your work will be covered during your maternity leave and how you will reenter your job.

- **If possible, don't begin a new job and a pregnancy at the same time.** Develop a track record first. If you make yourself indispensable, your peers and supervisors are more likely to accept your decisions about work and family.

- **When you return from a maternity leave or begin a reduced work schedule, devote special attention to staying in touch with the informal channels of communication in your organization.** Otherwise, lack of information may become a professional hazard.

- **Don't make the mistake of underestimating the impact—whether legitimate or merely perceived—of any absence from work.** Well-planned and clearly communicated job coverage, periodic check-ins while away, and careful negotiation with your boss can minimize any inconvenience created by your absence.

- **Let your own instinct be your guide.** Refuse to be bullied or worn down by insensitive colleagues. You will have fewer future regrets.

- **Remember that it may take more than one try to find a work setting that supports both your professional and personal goals.**

CHAPTER TWO

♦ ♦ ♦

Careers and Children: Not a Perfect Fit

Q: What would have made combining a family and career easier for you?
A: Being born a man.
—HARVARD BA 1967, HARVARD MEDICAL SCHOOL 1971,
MOTHER OF FOUR

No other group of women appear, on paper, to be as much like men in the professions as do the 902 Harvard women we surveyed. With credentials from the country's top colleges and graduate schools, they rank high in earning power, ambition, independence, and professional achievement. Yet their definition of "having it all" differs sharply from the way their husbands, fathers, and male colleagues have combined profession and family. When these women talk to their younger female colleagues about the work/family dilemma, sadly enough they pass on advice no one would ever give to a man, but which reflects the realities of penalties imposed only on women:

• • •

A Boston MBA and mother of three, who has just "geared down" to a four-day, 40-hour week, says, "I think one has to be realistic. Not all jobs can be combined with having children." Another MBA mom, discouraged by the tension from both her boss and her secretary (who "admit that they dislike children"), says that "neutrality, rather than support, is the best I have found." She passes this advice on to her younger colleagues, "Don't marry. Don't have children—if you wish to have a truly gratifying professional career."

• • •

An unmarried MBA, who has passionate feelings about the dichotomy between careers and children, believes that unless mothers *have* to work out of financial necessity, they are selfish to continue their careers. "A child should come first, and if a woman's not willing to sacrifice a bit (i.e., trade down from a BMW to a Chevy), then she shouldn't have them."

• • •

Susan Estrich, the first woman president of the *Harvard Law Review*, and now a working mother, reflects: "Mine was the first generation that thought—just maybe— that if we worked twice as hard and twice as long, we could have it all. And we did get more choices. But we have done better at playing according to the men's rules than changing them to our own."[1]

• • •

Working mothers should *not* be forced to the extreme of having to choose either careers or children. Women whose high goals and intelligence led them into the most demanding professions believed that the other pieces of their identities would fall neatly into place, as they did for men. Career women with children were rare in previous generations, so there was no one to caution that women cannot easily accept the traditional male rules of the game. An executive vice-president and mother of two says that there would have been fewer "surprises" in the work/family merger if "a few thousand more women had preceded me." Dr. Laura Tosi comments: "I'm in a field in which there are very few women and, unfortunately, very few mentors who are willing to help women. Thus, I've constantly felt that it takes me 10 times longer to figure out anything and everything!"

A physician told us that only one thing could have made combining a family and career easier for her: "Different role expectations for *men*."

NOT LIKE THE MEN

Except for World War II, when women were needed to work in factories, previous generations encouraged women to stay at home and rear their children. The Donna Reed generation played supermom in the home and the community, but their chief identity was usually a reflection of the support they provided their husbands, the family providers. Many of the relatively small number of women who did enter professions remained single or childless.

Changing Patterns

The first generation of mothers working in the professions— the Traditionalists—were mainly college-educated women who started careers relatively late, when their children were grown or in high school. They experienced the women's movement just as their daughters and sons were launching their own professional lives. These women supported their daughters' quest for both careers and children, and encouraged them to believe that they could have it all.

Trained on equal footing with the men, the next generation of career women—the Trailblazers—entered professions, certain that neither gender nor childbearing would be a barrier to their careers. If they faced conflicts between their two incompatible roles, they were reluctant to talk about them.

Because there was no defined place for mothers of young children in the work culture, the Trailblazers had no choice but to organize their lives around their professions. They studied harder than the men who sat next to them in graduate school. They knew that, to prove themselves on the job, they would have to outshine the men in the office. These women made the sacrifices in family life that have always been expected of men in fast-track careers.

Today's generation of mothers in the professions, the Achievers, are speaking out about the tension between their maternal and professional roles. Their voices are stronger because of their confidence in their abilities and because of new strains in feminist thought that urge women not to neglect personal fulfillment and maternal feelings. When we asked Cindy Horowitz, division chief financial officer for Citibank and a mother of two, if she has made significant personal sacrifices for the sake of her career, she replied, "I refuse to. I know it doesn't pay off in the long run unless it is your policy to do so all the time." She suggests that women take control of their personal decisions, and advises, "Know the trade-offs and make conscious decisions. Don't let the trade-offs just happen. They may not be the ones you would deliberately make."

The Achievers, termed *postfeminists* by some, are women accustomed to being in control—of their careers, their priorities, and their professional egos. They consciously chose careers that require 100 percent commitment, and they carefully planned the timing of their childbearing. The Achievers differ from the Trailblazers, who felt that they had no choice but to sacrifice family life for careers, and from the Traditionalists, who approached family and career sequentially, concentrating on only one at a time.

Now the Achievers are asking, must professional women follow traditional male career paths if they want to succeed and advance? And on the home front, what kind of support is needed from their spouses? How can the mold for women as primary nurturers be broken to expand the roles which men assume?

Today's generation, the Achievers, is left to struggle individually, without models for how a dual-career marriage can or should function. Studies such as *The Second Shift* point to the continuing imbalance between men and women in which responsibilities at home continue to be a heavier burden for women, regardless of salary, hours worked, or level of position.[2]

"In the last 20 years, working women nearly doubled their hours at the office or in the factory, while the numbers of hours they devote to child care and housework decreased by only 14 percent. During the same period, the total hours men put in at work and at home *fell* by 8 percent."[3]

The media are just beginning to target the new version of the dual-career couple, in which the husband is as frazzled and torn by multiple roles as is his wife. A Boston commercial for a late newscast showed dinner boiling over on the stove as children run through a room that is hurriedly being vacuumed. As the door opens, a *woman* walks in, briefcase in hand, and calls out, "Hi, honey. Dinner ready yet?"

A doctor at Brigham and Women's Hospital in Boston, married for the second time, suggests, "Marry only men who are equal domestic partners. And I don't mean men who 'help' you."

Professional women seem to spend much more time than their husbands worrying about whether their career is hurting their children. Many also feel torn by a social conscience that tells them they could be making a real contribution to society, instead of pursuing the good life, the fast track, and the corner office.

Business periodicals offer perpetual ratings of who is earning more than whom in corporate America. Many women, however, hold a different measure of success. One business school professor and mother of three observed:

"Women are now being sucked into the same trap that men have always found themselves in—'If you're so smart, why aren't you rich or famous?' For men, the excuse is, you're either lazy or stupid; for women, it's because you want to be a mother. Instead of pursuing the 'vanity of earthly wishes,' it seems to me we should put greater emphasis and value on the 'other' things people do in their lives—like being good parents, responsible and caring sons and daughters, little league coaches, voices in the choir, good neighbors. Our communities and indeed the human race depend more on the balanced lives of many people than it does on the achievements of a few superstars."

A psychiatrist, self-employed in Boston and formerly on an intense academic research track, accepts with some regret the professional price she paid for having children, but concludes: "I'd rather have my two beautiful children than any professorship."

When women first entered the male-dominated professions of business, law, and medicine, they visibly demonstrated their buy-in to the male work ethic by looking and acting as much like the men as they could. Conservative gray flannel suits and silk ties were their camouflage, symbols of their desire to fit in easily and without fanfare. They recognized that "image" is a powerful component to succeeding in the workplace.

Story Landis, the first professor in Harvard's Neurobiology Department to bear a child, felt the burden of being a "test case" for future mothers in the laboratory. "It seemed important to ensure that Michael's birth didn't change my identity too drastically; becoming a mother didn't preclude being a scientist."[4]

The Double Standard

Women with the same credentials as their male counterparts say they are still judged by different standards at work. A woman is "power hungry"; a man is a leader. A woman is "aggressive"; a man is just doing his job. One Boston lawyer and mother of a three-month-old observes, "Male attorneys with small babies are supportive. Others clearly think I am too 'tough' to be a good mother—I'm not like their wives!"

Dr. Andrea Franklin has learned to see the humor in her male colleagues' difficulty in accepting her toughness in the operating room. She recounted, with a hearty laugh, a comment one of her partners made to her husband: "Andrea is a great doctor, but I could never be married to her. She has bigger balls than I do!"

While they hear conflicting voices from within and from those around them, today's professional women are no longer choosing the traditional male pattern of roles devoted almost exclusively to career, as did their predecessors, the Trailblazers.

They continue to seek solutions for fulfillment rather than remain trapped in the stress and conflict that is still the price they pay for their dedication to a career and their love for their families. A lawyer for the United Nations, who has her feet planted in two cultures, talks of support from one and discrimination from the other. Her comfort and confidence as a working mother are fortified by her family background and culture: "Women in Africa have worked full-time and raised families for generations. That is what I grew up with and what my children are growing up with. It is our way of life." But when this mother of three, who works 60 hours a week, talks about the U.S. work culture, she emphasizes: "I think you pay a price for being a woman—period. The rate of upward mobility for women, regardless of having children or not, is much slower than that of men."

The current generation of women—the group we call the

Achievers—was expected to find the simple solution to balancing work and family. Instead, today's professional women are searching for answers, few of which seem simple. The glass ceiling, plus the maternal wall, heighten the tension for women trying to be professionals and mothers at the same time.

Based on the 902 surveys and 52 personal interviews, a portrait of the 1990s working mother emerges:

- She holds no doubt that superwoman is dead, but she sees no clear replacement to help manage her competing roles.

- She is paying an extraordinarily high price for her decision to be a mother as well as a professional. She doesn't quite fit the traditional roles at home or at work.

- She no longer wants to be like the men in her profession.

- Her children are her highest priority. She also values her marriage and recognizes the potentially fragile balance in dual-career couples.

- She is physically exhausted and tired of fighting seemingly never-ending battles for equality in the office.

- Her generation has no road maps for navigating its multiple roles.

A TURNING POINT

Feminist history has reached another turning point, which needs to be addressed. Women do want to go home, at least before 7:00 P.M. each night, but this goal often plays their ambition against their desire to nurture. MBA Priscilla Vincent refers to her need "to find my other self I had put on the shelf."

A California cardiologist wrote, "The feminist movement did women a great disservice by minimizing the rewards of child-rearing and denigrating its labors."

A 43-year-old Boston attorney says of the work/family dilemma: "It *is* getting better! But only at geologic pace."

A recent *Time*/CNN poll reported that "helping women balance work and family" is the top concern for the women's movement. What suffers most when women try to have it all? The poll results revealed that: children suffered 42 percent; marriage, 28 percent; and career, 12 percent as a result of the quest to have it all.[5]

Some women admit deep resentment toward their husbands, whose clear-cut roles somehow allow them to set aside time to exercise during the week or to play golf on the weekend. Many of today's working mothers have little time or energy for their mates, and virtually none for themselves. All of the women we met put "self" at the bottom of their long list of priorities. Fatigue has become the unfortunate trademark for today's working mother. Many women are simply exhausted from trying to fulfill all their roles and to do what is the impossible for any parent, regardless of gender. When we asked one Boston physician whether she has been successful at merging work and family, she replied, "Yes, but with decreased expectations on all fronts and chronic fatigue."

Because they have so little time to spend with their friends or in quiet conversation with other working mothers, many women think that they are alone in their dilemma. They do not realize that women across the country—and even in their own offices—share their feelings and frustrations.

The first step in untangling the contradictions of the 1990s woman is to understand her. This chapter introduces the common voices and themes expressed by the 902 women we surveyed. In subsequent chapters, their personal stories, grouped by life choices, will reveal the complexity of women's contemporary roles and offer unique and surprising solutions for women *and* men who seek a better balance between profession and family.

THE SEDUCTION OF THE BABY

Q: Have you made personal sacrifices for the sake of your career?
A: ''Leaving a three-month-old infant in another person's house for nine hours, five days a week is a personal sacrifice.''
—ALICE CORT, MD, MOTHER OF TWO

Most of the women we surveyed were entrenched in their careers when their children were born and were unprepared for what a former Harvard professor described as ''the seduction of the baby.'' Regardless of training and professional level, physicians, MBAs, and lawyers said they were caught off guard by the intensity of their desire to be with their children.

''My perspective on work has changed,'' says a former Wall Street investment manager. She is now self-employed so she can devote more time to her two children, one of whom has Down's syndrome. ''I remember once thinking I'd *never* not work in a traditional corporate environment.''

No measure of professional reward can equal the love and affection of a child, these feminists say. They want to excel as both mothers *and* lawyers, doctors, or businesswomen. Although most are doing both, many say that they doubt whether they are doing their best for their careers or their children. They also take seriously their ''investment'' in the next generation. Asked whether they are successfully combining family and career, we heard, ''The jury is still out,'' or ''I will tell you when my children are grown up and I am 80 without a divorce!'' One California physician, who purposely married a man with a lower key career, said: ''It's hard, but doable. No nervous breakdown yet!''

Only one factor—other than a 36-hour day—could have made combining career and children easier for her, said a neonatologist and mother of three: "Less personal guilt for the inability to be in two places at once."

A former consultant, now on leave from her international banking career, said, "Before age 28, I was not interested in having children, other than as a vague possibility in the future—which was just as well, because I was working very hard. After 28, biology took over, and I simply wanted a child (couldn't/can't explain why) so much that it dwarfed any feelings about work."

"Maternal instinct" and the biological difference between women and men have been the centuries-old excuse for discriminating against women—the excuse for excluding women from medical school, for segregating them from the men in college, for denying them promotions in business. Women continue to fight the "weaker sex" stereotype when they take maternity leaves, reduce their working hours, or refuse job-related travel—all because they want to find a way to spend more time with their children.

Two-thirds of the 902 women who responded to our survey said their careers had *no influence* on their decisions about whether or not to have children. However, career demands did affect *when* they became parents. Some decided to have only one child, as a response to the daunting logistics of merging professional and family responsibilities and to avoid further professional penalties.

• • •

One former MBA consultant for McKinsey and Company, now enrolled in a PhD program, comments: "I plan to limit the family size to one child to permit me to resume my career full-time. My switch to an academic career was compatible with my decision to remarry and work harder on this marriage than the first, which suf-fered from the Harvard Business School and consulting life-style."

• • •

A California physician, who reduced her hours from 80 to 60 a week after the birth of her daughter, said, "One of the main reasons I have only one child is so she will not have to divide the time we have together with another child."

• • •

A Texas attorney, whose bonuses have been reduced since she took a four-month maternity leave four years ago, worries about how she could manage her evening and weekend work if she had another child. "I'm not sure I could keep up the schedule I have now with a second child. The last time I took a maternity leave, I knew that I would pay for it financially for years to come."

• • •

The higher a woman rises professionally, the greater the conflict can become between work and home. "I miss my baby," a clinical instructor in cancer research said quietly. A United Nations official with a heavy travel schedule said she worries that "my daughter is more attached to the nanny than to me."

Women whose own mothers worked outside the home tend to feel less torn than they otherwise might. Renee Matalon, an attorney who grew up with a working mother, said, "My mother believed in girls being educated and in women being strong and independent. I didn't grow up thinking that a really good mother is home all the time. Neither did my husband—whose mother helped run a family-owned business."

Renee knows that her son will not suffer from the four days a week that she works, yet she also feels a strong maternal tug when she is away from him. "I'm just beginning to see that, to a child, a mother is the most important person in the world."

Even with an "incredibly involved" husband, Renee has observed that *she* is the one her son most wants at the end of the day. Unlike her husband, Renee feels tremendous guilt when she cannot leave work on time and has to miss dinner with her son.

She has done an about-face from her initial concern about how she thought she would turn out as a mother. "When I found out I was pregnant, I was weepy. I had this vision of myself as a dumpy, uninteresting person, feeling trapped for 20 years." Tall and elegant in her second pregnancy, Renee still has some doubts about whether she put the pieces of her life together in just the right way. On most days, however, "I am happy and feel more energetic than ever."

Society's Mixed Signals

Conflicting messages from society about what a mother *should* be doing pit one set of choices against another. Noted pediatrician T. Berry Brazelton suggests that even women who leave the work force for full-time motherhood are not immune from distress and confusion in their maternal roles. Women at home, he has observed, "are suffering almost as much as women in the work force. They're feeling deserted, left out, uncared for. They talk about how, if they go to the park, they're the only mother in the park; all the other people are baby-sitters, and they don't have anybody to talk to about how they feel."[6]

A Harvard MBA and mother of three told us how offended she was that we did not categorize parenting as "work" on our questionnaire. A full-time mother, who is considering reentering the work force after a 10-year break, she says she gets "no respect" for how she spends her days. "I '*work*' all day long: one, raising kids; two, holding leadership positions in the community and my church; three, lobbying for improvements in government. But not for pay!"

When—and under what circumstances—she will return to the office is often the crucial question for today's working mother. There is no single "right" length of time for a maternity leave. A minority of women feel physically and psychologically ready to return to work immediately. Nine women took no maternity leave at all. Many prefer a three- or four-month leave to bond with their new baby. Eighty-two percent of the mothers we surveyed took a maternity leave of four months or less. Of this group, 28 percent took two months off and 25 percent, three months. Some women need extra time, particularly if their babies are born with health problems.

• • •

A California lawyer, who took an 8-week leave with her first child and 14 weeks with her second, said, "I really felt as though I *knew* my second baby when I went back to work; my first was a stranger to me for months."

• • •

A law professor, who took no leave with her first child because she had just started a new job, and none with her second because she was being evaluated for tenure, had similar feelings. "The intimacy of my relationship with my third child exceeds that with the other two. I took a year—one semester of maternity leave and one semester of leave without pay. It was heaven!"

• • •

Women with older children were quick to dismiss the myth that getting back to a fast-paced profession is easy once children enter elementary school. Many, in fact, said their lives became more hectic when their children began to participate in after-school activities to which they needed to be driven and in which they wanted their parents to watch them perform.

"Quality time" is another myth that did not pass the reality test for many women in our survey.

• • •

A Harvard MBA, who abandoned a Fortune 500 company for self-employment and more time with her children, said, "How children do in school, with peers, in activities and sports is difficult to assess when the parents get home at 8:00 P.M. and [the children] are in their pajamas. As much as we want it to be otherwise, children may require parental involvement at 3:30 P.M. Being home in time for kissing them good-night does not a successful family make."

She also told the story of her best friend, a lawyer working full-time in New York City. "She enrolled her three-year-old son in a 7:30 P.M. Gymboree class. Every Wednesday night, she'd put him in the car to drive to the class. Every Wednesday night, he'd fall asleep en route. Finally, in desperation, she heard herself say to Ben, 'Wake up. It's quality time!' She quit work with her second child and now has a fledgling law practice while raising her three kids."

• • •

In some ways, it is easier to take an infant to day care than to disappoint an older child by missing her basketball game. However, pediatrician Brazelton suggests that parents place their children at risk if they convey guilt and ambivalence as they leave for work. Children are quick to pick up and readily absorb these negative emotions, even if they are perfectly happy with their day care, Brazelton concludes.[7]

He also has observed that mothers who feel confident about their decision to work pass their assurance on to their children.

However, he remains deeply concerned about the damage our work-obsessed culture is inflicting on family life—for parents as well as for children.

• • •

MBA Barbara Pearce admits, "I sometimes still lie about where I am when my baby-sitter is off. It doesn't help things a whole lot if men act like there is something wrong or bad about integrating home and work. And men don't do it, for the most part. You see men doing the dropoffs at the nursery school, but seldom do you see them doing the pickups."

• • •

Even with the best-laid plans, mothers are at high risk for a collision of roles when the unexpected occurs. Typical childhood illnesses, such as chicken pox or the flu, can wreak havoc on women who cannot be in two places at once and whose husbands do not help with sick-child care. Many also find that sick children bring little sympathy in the workplace. Even in progressive companies that offer on-site sick-child care or subsidize in-home care, the problem is not really solved. Sick children want a parent or, at the very least, someone they know well to comfort them. Mothers cannot be at their most productive when they feel worried, guilty, and angry for not being permitted to do what they believe is the right thing.

• • •

A Boston attorney says, with regret, "My son has been sent to school with a slight temperature because there was no other solution. (And I would wait for the call from school.) It stresses both the marriage and the job. I have found the best solution is to leave the office and claim another appointment—the less known the better.

"I have gone to work sick to save sick days for when my son is sick. And I know other working mothers who have done the same. In fact, we end up using *less* sick time than others."

• • •

High achievers cannot stop comparing and evaluating themselves in each of their roles for which there are few current road maps. "I do less work than my colleagues," says an assistant professor of medicine, "and less mothering than my mother. And I have no time of my own." A 1991 *Working Mother* survey of 3,000 women reported that 85 percent of the respondents "confess that they are the key perpetuators of their own guilt," while 92 percent "say they are proud of their ability to provide for their families." Three-quarters of the women also acknowledged that their job has improved their self-esteem and encouraged their children to be more independent.[8]

An MBA, who left investment banking for part-time work in academia when her second child was born, says, "You cannot have it all. If you have children, ask yourself what is a 'good' mother. Be sure to sustain the level *you* define as 'good.' Otherwise, your guilt will preclude you from enjoying the time you *can* spend with your children."

STIFLING THE INNER VOICE

"Which is more important to you, your field or your children?" the department head asked.

She replied, "That's like asking me if I could walk better if you amputated my right leg or my left leg."[9]

• • •

A New York attorney summarizes the good news and the bad news. "The men view me as their equal in the workplace. They also expect me to have a lesser involvement with my children and family life—as though I have a 'wife' to run things at home. So I should have no concerns to cloud my head during the workday or evening."

• • •

A Maryland surgeon recalls being told in her interview for a residency in plastic surgery that the first woman in the program had quit and that no one could ever have a baby and be in the program. She did enter, did have a baby, and did work 100-plus hours a week alongside all the men. She now works 60 hours a week in surgery, in what she considers a "lower key job."

No one can perform a starring role as both parent and professional, she says. She accepts that she is doing "about 80 percent" of what she would like in each of her roles, and reconciles her trade-offs: "(1) I'm a worse mother because I'm not at home; (2) I'm a worse doctor because I'm a mom; (3) I wouldn't have it any other way."

• • •

A California lawyer switched from a partnership track to a 35-hour week in corporate law after her second child was born. She continues to feel ambivalent about the balance between motherhood and profession, and explains what she has given up: "My career has progressed slowly; my personal time has vanished; my children have spent more time with others than I would like."

Her husband "just knew" that he would never help much with child care, she says. Their two toddlers are happy and well adjusted, "but I'm a nervous wreck."

• • •

Careers and children are *not* a perfect fit, even though the potential is there for a smoother alliance. Professional women who also choose motherhood risk a loss of confidence and optimism for merging their dual roles as they face cruel tests nearly every day. Older male colleagues with "traditional" families mutter that women should really be at home with their children—yet chastise them for wanting to leave work on time to attend their child's birthday party.

Some of the smartest women in the country said that they're too embarrassed to attend their reunions at Harvard Business School if they have dropped out of the work force, left the fast track by choosing part-time work, or decided to follow anything other than the standard male career path.

A corporate vice-president, married, but not planning to have children, carries vivid images of her 10th Harvard Business School reunion a few years ago. "The most striking fact was how exhausted the women with children were. Their number one priority was their children; number two was the job; number three was their husband; and a very distant last was themselves."

Self-blame can also take a severe toll on women who already have far too much stress in their daily lives. What stands in the way of balancing work and family? "Myself," answered a Boston physician. "I expect too much of myself in all areas."

Married women said they want their marriages—so different from their parents' and their husbands' parents'—to succeed, but the territory of dual-career couples remains uncharted. As much as their husbands wanted to marry intelligent women with careers of their own, they admitted disappointment for not having a "wife." Add the possible power struggles over whose career comes first, and the potential for marital strife intensifies.

• • •

A surgeon and mother of two, expecting her third child, is aware of how much time devotion to a career demands. "Schedule in your husband and children, or they'll be bumped," she advises.

• • •

A radiologist, married to a self-employed architect, appreciates the flexible schedule her husband has to assist with child-rearing. She, however, is the family's main breadwinner and regrets that financial pressure restricts her own flexibility. "I am not sure that I have the right priorities," she says. "Will this have an impact plus or minus on my children—my marriage? Will I have any regrets in the future?"

• • •

One MBA marketing director offered this advice: "At 25, try to 'talk' to your 35-year-old self. Figure out what she will want so you can plan or at least anticipate how to satisfy her when you meet her. Don't run the risk that she will resent you for having tunnel vision."

• • •

The women we met were high achievers throughout their academic careers, yet many have lost faith in what they first valued professionally.

• • •

A successful Washington, D.C., attorney, waiting to have children until she makes partner, said, "I believe that being a lawyer is a *terrible* career choice for women because there is so little flexibility in hours. It is only good for people with no outside interests, friends, or family. I could not recommend it to *any* woman who is married or who wants to have children, unless she is willing to take a low-status, low-paying position with no possibility for advancement."

• • •

In a speech at her alma mater, Dr. Donna Whitney described stifling her own inner voice when her survival as a medical student depended on it: "From the beginning of my medical education, I was aware of a tension, or incompatibility, between the unspoken assumptions of the profession and my own equally unspoken values. . . . I went through medical school with a vague, nagging, and unsettling sense of being out of step, out of place, and out of my element. . . . My judging and my way of knowing were different from the dominant mode. These flashes of realization were brief, but not comforting, and I continued through school feeling silent and invisible much of the time, with occasional episodes of sticking out like a sore thumb."[10]

• • •

Alice Richmond, an MBA who has always worked full-time while rearing her three children, came up with her own strategy for participating in a corporate world that would never acknowledge the importance of her parenting role. "I had to take the attitude of 'I'm going to have this career and I'm going to be pregnant while I'm doing it, and I dare the company to get in my way or hinder me.' " Alice describes the "threatened boys out there who are waiting for their opportunity to show that women don't belong" and her concern, as the only woman in a professional position in her company, that "discussing parenting issues in my work environment results in having some jerk trying to use the information against you. If I had the choice *now*, I would leave the corporate environment completely. Not to be a house-wife or traditional mother, but just because its rewards no longer outweigh its constant requirement for a vigilant attitude toward the men who are my peers. In my twenties and thirties, I had the strength and will to fight. I believed I could win. At forty, I can't understand what prize I thought I'd be winning. If it was self-assurance, I got what I wanted. If it was independence, self-reliance, and confidence, I got that too.

"Now what else is the corporation offering? It's hard to get excited about bashing your head against a glass ceiling. Every time you pull back to take a running start at it, you see your own reflection.

"And then you say, 'So what?' and go back to your Hyatt Regency Club Frequent Flyer upgrade hotel room and write a novel on your laptop computer."

Deciding to learn "their" rules but play by her own, Alice used her heavy travel schedules to write a novel during airplane trips and hotel stopovers. She says of her accomplishment as a writer, "It helps to have a 'backup' image."

• • •

Feeling successful as a parent can also boost a woman's self-image and focus her mind clearly on the true prizes in life. An MBA, now working part-time, reflects, "Without a child, I probably would have been a vice-president with an ulcer by now." She advises women who are trying to sort out work/family choices, "Decide first with your heart, then your head.

Your head can always devise a way to accommodate the needs of your heart, but rarely does it work in reverse. And if you're not happy, nothing you do will turn out right."

Many women call themselves lucky if they can reach any version of balance between career and children, recognizing that entrenched social roles and a rigid work culture are pulling against them.

Lena Zezulin, a mother of two and part-time law partner working 30 hours a week, offered her formula: (1) a spouse who will also work part-time; (2) limited financial goals for the childbearing years; (3) clients who do not require 24-hour-a-day litigation; (4) an accommodating senior law partner; (5) a home close to the Metro. Her footnote: "Take away any one of these and I might not cope."

The most intriguing story we heard of the hoops women will jump through to meet the demands of a dual-career marriage came from Scandinavia. A Harvard MBA, who married a classmate from Norway, commuted *weekly* for four years, with her child, from her job in Denmark to her husband in Norway. She explained, "I loved my job with my company and was totally committed!" When her second child was born, she decided to stop working for a few years. "As much as I loved my career, I realized I also wanted the personal fulfillment that comes from sharing time with your spouse and children."

We heard other stories of logistical nightmares endured by women determined to succeed in each of their competing roles. Many women said they regret they have no extended family nearby to provide support. An assistant professor of medicine, often required to work long hours in her laboratory, relies on her mother to travel *700 miles* "to help at times of a crunch."

A former high-powered international consultant, with a six-figure income, recently began the switch to academia for a chance at a calmer life-style. Her advice: "Establish your own criteria of success in life. It's difficult for 'women like us' to wean ourselves from externally validated criteria such as position, income, etc., and focus on internal criteria we measure ourselves against. We have to *give ourselves points* for being concerned parents, participating in community action, or whatever else is important to us."

The stories of these Harvard women reflect the extent to which women's roles are shaped by our personal history even when, intellectually, we want to take a different path. The women's stories reflect high standards for every aspect of their lives, and the sense that, regardless of the "package" they put together for profession and family, there will be trade-offs. A professor of law who decided to say "the hell with it about work stuff and follow my heart" received tenure while raising three children, but gave up on scholarly research due to time constraints. "Some think I'm lazy and unproductive," she says. "Others can't understand how I get everything done." And the subjective perceptions of those doing the judging often influence who gets the job assignments, mentors, and first consideration for promotion.

At least the issues are out on the table now. The current generation of working mothers is no longer afraid to disclose that they sometimes feel a deep tension between their careers and their children. Some women (and men) are beginning to tell the truth at work about leaving early occasionally for a child's piano recital or soccer game. When someone asks a mother how she feels after being up all night with a sick child, many would now admit, "I'm exhausted." And that admission in no way denotes a weaker sex. Dveera Segal, a mother of three who practiced law for 10 years, advises younger women: "You cannot do everything at 100 percent of your standards. You must be clear about your priorities and act accordingly. You *can* balance a professional and personal life. Each will lose something in the balance and each will gain something from the other."

Women are beginning to speak loud and clear: There is absolutely no good reason why careers and children should be destined for a collision course. They talk of how their children have made them better people by helping to both clarify and enrich the judgment and ethics they bring to their roles in the office.

A lawyer working a reduced schedule of 30 hours a week reflected: "For many years, I worked impossible hours with all of my 'personal life' subject to the job. My husband and I went into counseling after every big case." She now tells other women:

"I know having the children has made me a better person and even a better lawyer. Maybe someone who was less compulsive about life would have an easier time of it, but I seem to be stuck with myself. Since you end up paying a price professionally no matter when you have children, you should probably have them when you are ready. If you do what seems right and persist, I believe it all works out. Law firms dissolve, specialties dry up, mentors disappear. However, no one and nothing takes away the sloppy, wet kisses and hugs."

The first step in finding a solution is to know the problem. That is the purpose of this book. Our survey indicates that women are beginning to emerge from the tremendous confusion that has clouded each of their many roles. Today's professional women are coming forward to say that what is wrong with today's family life is not their fault. They are less likely to apologize for being themselves and for making their own choices about balancing work and family. They have begun to create a new identity for the role of parent/professional. We cannot yet predict the outcome of the stories about to be told. We know we are seeing the beginnings of a new chapter in the history of working women.

Through personal stories and real-life strategies, *Women and the Work/Family Dilemma* will address the following questions:

- **Why do women feel more conflicted than men when they are not with their children?** Are women's values about what is important in life really so different from men's?

- What kind of support is necessary, in the office and in the home, for a smoother alliance between profession and family?

- What strategies are successful for dismantling the maternal wall?

- How have today's professional women begun to forge a new identity for those with strong career ambitions who also want to be successful parents?

CHAPTER THREE

◆ ◆ ◆

Superwoman:
Myth or Reality?

The myth of superwoman has hung on long after the media stopped airing fantasy-based commercials about working women's lives:

● ● ●

Here she comes, home from the office after 12 hours of high-powered negotiations in the executive suite. Her designer suit is still fresh and unwrinkled; her face radiant and unlined as she opens her arms to greet her two adorable children—and sends a seductive glance toward her handsome husband, beaming proudly in the background.

Watch her as, with one smooth motion, she slips off her jacket and into a dainty apron as she glides toward the spotless kitchen to create a three-course meal for her beloved family. After dinner she will check the children's French homework and read them a chapter of *Jane Eyre* before tucking the little cherubs into bed.

While her husband watches the late-night news, she will disappear into the den to make an overseas call that will clinch a multinational deal for her company.

● ● ●

Who *is* this irritating creature? Why does her suit never wrinkle and her smile never waver? Why does her house never need vacuuming and her family never eat frozen pizza? Why doesn't her husband get off his duff and help her? Why is superwoman smiling?

Perhaps even the advertising world finally figured out the unreality of the vision they had chosen to portray. Many of these commercials portrayed women who were almost defiant in their quest to prove that they could have it all. Often, before the image dissolved to a closeup of the product, superwoman would thrust her perfectly manicured fist skyward and burst into feminist song, "Yes, I am woman—W-O-M-A-N!"

Anyone who has ever tried to live up to this image of professional and personal perfection knows that only defiance—coupled with the ability to survive on very little sleep—can motivate a woman to do what no man has ever done. How many men are pressured to succeed as both primary parent and career fast-tracker, with no trade-offs, no compromises, and no sacrifices at work or at home?

Although the superwoman commercials have bitten the dust, many women are still accepting this exhausting model, particularly at work. They think they must behave as if they have no family obligations or they will be considered weak and unable to cope.

It is a mistake for any woman to measure her own success by the standards of a media creation. Even women whose real lives closely reflect the superwoman ideal know the truth. There are trade-offs between career and family.

THE NEW FAST-TRACKERS

The women we portray in this chapter have done extremely well at setting aside guilt, regret, and ambivalence about the choices they have made. These fast-trackers are among the fortunate few who have broken through the glass ceiling. They see their lives clearly and have set their own standards for work and for family. They firmly refuse to let others set the rules for them.

We acknowledge that they are not typical people. These women work 50-plus hours a week and are in the running for the top positions in their fields. They are fueled by solid professional confidence and intense personal drive. Their family lives are secure, and they can afford the best help money can buy. They set a personal and professional pace that is exhausting even to watch. Few of us live this way, but we all can learn from them.

These women prove it is not true that "fast-tracker" must mean superbitch, supercool, unfeeling, and distant from the needs of her family. The women we interviewed are warm and caring individuals. They founded their careers on a plan and a purpose. They thrive on the fast-forward rush of their lives. From day one, their careers have been on track, undeterred even by pregnancy and motherhood.

They rely on an equal partnership at home—but they also have broken new ground in the office. These women refuse to allow their work culture, no matter how traditional or immovable, to consume all of their time and most of their energy. They have developed new plans that allow them to get their work done and still see their families.

Karen Green moves with ease through the 60-hour weeks she puts in as a senior partner in the Boston law office of Hale and Dorr. Because she grew up in a household in which both of her parents worked long hours, she carries very little guilt about being a busy working mother.

"I think I'm very lucky. I had the benefit of having a mother who *had* to work. She's a very smart lady, but she didn't have the opportunities I've had. I grew up in a working-class community. The whole time I was growing up, I watched my parents accommodating each other. My mother demonstrated toys in the evening while my father pumped gas in the daytime. Then my father joined the police force and my mother started substituting in parochial school. The nuns decided my mother had a real gift for kids and they struck a deal that, if she enrolled in college, she could teach full-time in the school. For 10 years she taught, went to school at night, and raised a family. I can remember getting up in the middle of the night and seeing my mother at the kitchen table writing a paper. I admired my mother. I never felt she was neglecting me. And she was always the first person at a PTA meeting."

At the time her first child was born, Karen was doing a stint in the U.S. Attorney's Office in Boston, where both staff and budget are quite lean, and where taking a maternity leave longer than three months would place too heavy a burden on the other lawyers. Karen knows how good she has it at Hale and Dorr, where the size of the firm and the tone from the top allowed her to take a six-month maternity leave with her second child.

Since the birth of her second child two years ago, Karen made senior partner and has actually increased her work hours. "I could not live the way I do without live-in help. My schedule is simply too unpredictable." In her senior role in her firm, Karen is very aware of the need to pull her weight. "Although I like to think that things are changing now, I have not reduced my hours of work because my sense has been that it is detrimental to a woman's career in the litigation area."

Right now, 11 of the 86 senior partners at Hale and Dorr are women; of the 40 junior partners, 14 are women. "Having more women attorneys has made this a better place. I want there to be more women. It's important to be role models for other women—to be accepted in the profession—and not as a second-class citizen."

As we interview Karen in her elegant office with a panoramic view of the Boston skyline, she tells us: "The thing I love about Hale and Dorr is that the firm really encourages people to be the people they are." For Karen, being her own person translates into serving as a director of a children's trust fund and as a member of the state's Judicial Nominating Committee.

Like all working mothers, Karen suffers occasional self-doubt about how much she has on her plate, and admits: "My life is extremely structured. Every once in a while, I feel like just taking off with my children and husband. There have been times when I'm cleaning my house on a Saturday night that I've wished I had a 9-to-5 job." Karen, however, tries to maintain a global perspective on her work/family merger, and says: "I don't view my children as 'costing' me. I can't imagine life without them and would never suggest that anyone should forgo parenting for a career."

Like many of the women we met who work a "full-time plus" schedule, Karen has established certain family rituals. "We have an unwritten rule that one parent is always at home until 8:00 in the morning and one parent is home by 6:30 at night. Whenever I have to travel for a case, I always call at breakfast time, even if it means getting up at 4:00 A.M. in Portland, Oregon." If Karen has to work on a weekend, she goes into her office at 5:00 A.M. and returns home about 9:00 A.M.—often before her children are even out of bed.

As we notice the children's artwork decorating her door and the photographs of her children proudly displayed next to her law books, Karen tells us about her family: "My husband is my biggest cheerleader. And my six-year-old is very much like my husband. When I say to him, 'Gee Colin, I'm sorry I'm not going to be home on time tonight,' he says, 'That's OK, Mom. I just need to know what time you're coming home.' "

Karen and her husband, a real estate lawyer at a Boston bank, make it a point to schedule regular discussions about their shared balance between profession and family. Has the pendulum swung too much toward one to the detriment of the other? Is one parent spending too many hours away from the family? Is the division of household responsibilities gender neutral?

Both Karen and her husband believe strongly in her mother's wise counsel: "Just do what you know is right and be true to yourself." And then Karen adds, "I think you can waste a lot of time and energy feeling guilty."

THE CORNER OFFICE

Joyce Fensterstock, MBA class of 1973, is one of only two presidents of mutual funds companies and one of two women in senior management at PaineWebber. Petite, charismatic, and elegantly dressed, Joyce conducts business from her 15th-floor corner office. She has broken through Wall Street's glass ceiling where, she says, "Women are simply not welcome at senior levels."

She began her career in the lucrative field of investment banking, but its mandatory travel time prompted her to move into mutual fund management for a schedule more compatible with her personal life. How does she manage a family *and* a $20 billion family of mutual funds? Joyce has learned to separate profession and home into two mental compartments, to which she devotes her full attention—one at a time.

"I do not encourage business calls in the evening unless it is a true emergency. I know that whatever is happening at 10:00 P.M. can wait until morning. And I refuse to discuss work at home. This frustrates my husband, who believes that talking about work is a form of communication, but I'd rather talk about our children's lives."

Joyce begins her 60-hour week at PaineWebber at 7:30 A.M. and often ends with required business entertaining in the evening. She reserves another 20 hours for time with her three children, ages eight, six, and three, whose photographs she proudly displays on her uncluttered mahogany desk.

With the help of two nannies, Joyce has every family contingency fully covered. However, she is the one who sits, clapping in the audience, at her children's school plays, takes them to the doctor, and brings them to school on their first day.

Despite her well-established track record on Wall Street and a boss who appreciates the value of family life, Joyce admits, "I don't talk about family issues at work unless it's critical to do so. Their doctor appointments become *my* appointments. If I need to go to a teacher's conference in the morning, I simply call in to say I'll be an hour late. I figure it's nobody's business and it can only hurt professionally to talk about it."

Joyce is among the few women in her profession who have a mentor—another key to her success, she says. "This is an environment where it's high risk for a man to mentor a woman. Men look to groom clones of themselves. And there just aren't enough women on Wall Street to mentor other women."

Joyce has also tackled a new project: "Me. As part of my midlife crisis, I finally realized that I was not going to be any good to anyone if I did not take the time to do something just for myself. I now reserve the time it takes to exercise three times a week."

Joyce and her husband are comfortable with the balance she has found between work and family. Their children are happy and well adjusted. Yet even a woman as clear and confident about her life choices as she is not entirely immune from the penalties imposed by role expectations held by others. Every once in a while, Joyce feels tested by women who have chosen a different life-style.

Recently, the mother of one of her child's school friends announced that her child would never be allowed to play with someone who spent so many hours with a nanny. On one level, Joyce knows that her children are doing well. On another, she cannot help but feel hurt that her own child's play group has been limited by one nonworking mother's judgment about the best way to rear children.

SETTING A PERSONAL TIMETABLE

A few of the fast-trackers we surveyed ignored tradition and started their families before establishing their careers. The choice was risky and, for some, meant turning down job offers that would have sent them up the corporate ladder more quickly. For these women, however, the trade-off was worth it. Family came first. A rewarding career paralleled the growth of their children.

From day one on the job, Ann Fudge, director of marketing and business development for Kraft General Foods, has acted without apology for being both a manager and a mother. With a soft-spoken style, Ann combines intense personal drive with an unwavering commitment to a secure and happy marriage and family life.

Since her graduation from Harvard Business School in 1977, Ann has set professional goals with a personal timetable. She has been married for nearly 20 years; her two sons, now teenagers, were born before she entered business school.

As she answered our questions, Ann ate a spartan lunch of fruit salad and popcorn at her desk in her corner office in White Plains, N.Y., and apologized for signing overdue paperwork.

"Because I established family as my first priority very early on, my decisions about career were fairly easy," she said. Following her own timetable has meant saying no to several career offers that did not fit with her personal plans.

In 1986—two years ahead of her game plan—Ann was in line for promotion to general manager at General Mills. But she left her position in the Midwest to accept a job at General Foods because it offered the added benefit of putting her closer to her ill mother on the east coast. Recently she was offered a major position in another city. She declined again, to put family first.

"It would have meant relocating just as my son was entering his senior year in high school. I didn't think it would be right to move him that year. And I did not want to be a commuter wife and mom."

Ann is 39 now. Her long-held goal is to become general manager by age 40. She has one more year to go—and she fully expects to make it.

IN FULL CONTROL

We know that superwoman is a myth—but there *is* one truth buried under the fantasy trappings that surround her. Any woman working in a demanding profession and rearing a family somehow must find superhuman energy just to manage the logistics of it all.

Christine Letts, former commissioner of transportation for the state of Indiana and mother of two young children, relies on careful planning and efficient use of her time, at work and at home.

Christine decided to move from private industry to state government even though the switch meant a 40-percent cut in salary. One aspect of the trade-off was worth it: she reached a high enough level in state government to call the shots on how many meetings she attended and how efficiently they ran.

Her 60- to 70-hour week began at 6:30 A.M. each morning when she left for work. She capitalized on being an early morning person and felt fortunate to run an office where much of the action took place early in the day. She knows her family life would not fit well with a company whose work ethic was based on a 9:00 A.M. to 7:00 P.M. schedule.

Christine worked through most lunches, attended evening town meetings, held regular press conferences, and conducted tours of the state. However, she tried to spend from 6:00 to 8:00 P.M. at home, uninterrupted, with her husband and two children, ages five and eight.

Christine has worked hard to establish clear and shared goals with her boss and her husband. "I try to model healthy family behavior for others. I made it clear that evening meetings are not welcome unless absolutely necessary. I told my last boss that the only time I can see my kids is between 6:00 and 8:00 P.M., and that I'd prefer to go home, and come back to work after 8:00 P.M. if necessary."

She encouraged the people in her office to balance their lives and to make sure that they plan time for vacations. "I don't think it's a badge of courage *not* to take vacations. I think that's ridiculous. And if people need to leave early for family obligations, I don't look askance. I try to accommodate things like that."

Christine and her husband, David, follow a clearly defined plan for who does what at home. She says neither partner feels resentment or frustration for carrying a heavier load. Instead, they try to put aside professional egos to keep the household running smoothly. For example, her husband took an unpaid, two-month leave when their first child was born because, among other reasons, Christine was earning more money.

"We contract out cleaning and that kind of stuff," she says. "Neither one of us ends up doing things that take a lot of hours and that are real drudgery."

Like many working mothers, Christine handles a lot of the "administration" at home. "David did the face-to-face with the baby-sitter because I had a longer commute. I leave the notes for the baby-sitter. I leave David notes, too. I'm the control influence—probably to a fault."

Earlier in her career, Christine paid her dues without question, leaving her office about 7:00 P.M. each night and working on Saturdays and Sundays. "If I had not done that, I might not have developed credibility. When you're first starting out, you have to be prepared to sacrifice more rather than less. And you have to be flexible. If you walk into a situation and, all of a sudden, things don't fit, that's a signal that you didn't do a good job analyzing things ahead of time."

Christine has crisp priorities and sharp political instincts. Now that she has reached a high enough professional level, she can help make inroads for other women. In her no-nonsense style, she offers advice for women who are looking for a job that will be a good fit with a family life:

"There's a way of gathering information in an interview that's instructive about people's work schedules and their expectations for everyone else. One way is to ask a potential boss for a representative work calendar. Then ask for an interview with someone who's in a similar job, but wouldn't be supervising you. It's hard to ask whether bosses have a family life, but it's OK to ask peers and to talk about what their workdays are like."

Christine established 10 years of recognized professional performance before she began to negotiate the work plan for her job—on her terms. She tells other women to build up their bargaining chips and their professional credibility before they try to go after what they really want for the long term.

NO DOWNTIME

To combine profession and family, many successful women have learned to tune out everyone else's opinions and expectations about how they should be leading their lives.

Lisa Churchville manages all the details—from the critical to the seemingly minor—at work and at home by making every second count. Positive, upbeat, and energetic, Lisa is director of sales for an NBC affiliate in Chicago and the mother of two young children.

Her typical 60-hour workweek includes at least one extracurricular function: a sports event, a breakfast or dinner meeting. "Sometimes in a crunch time, I go home, put the kids to bed, and then go back to work. I can do this because I live a five-minute drive from work."

Lisa jumped ship from another network when she was given powerful signals that her status as a new parent had moved her to the "mommy track"—without cause or her consent. She cannot sing enough praise for NBC, because her station accepts and accommodates her need for a bit of flexibility as a working mother. Her children are four months and five years old.

"I'm able to take a lunch hour if I want to attend a school event. I don't hesitate to tell the truth about where I'm going. It is accepted and it isn't a problem. In my previous work environment, I *never* felt comfortable talking about my child or ever admitting I had to get home."

Becoming a parent has spurred her to become more efficient about her personal, family, and business life. "I work more efficiently. There is not a single moment when I'm not thinking about work, regardless of what I'm doing—even when I'm straightening up the house. It borders on hyperkinetic activity. No downtime. I walk to work and dictate on the way. I don't experience a high level of fatigue because I exercise regularly—swimming during my lunch hour."

At home Lisa uses her time management skills to stay on track. "I always shop by catalogue. I lay out my wardrobe for the week and write it down, so I don't have to waste time figuring out what's clean in my closet."

The real key to balancing work and family? "My husband. I can't fathom doing this without someone who is truly involved as a parent."

Her life is not perfectly balanced, however. "Unfortunately, I'm not making great friendships at this juncture of my life. My focus has to be my work. I just do it and am more productive for this clear and single-minded focus."

A MOTHER IN A MACHO WORK CULTURE

Considering her 80-hour workweek and the six-page list of her professional publications, it is difficult to believe that Dr. Ellen Downing believes she has slowed her career a bit for the sake of her children. However, she explains, "I slowed my research career for my children. I have also foreclosed professional options by refusing to travel on a regular basis."

Dr. Downing, has made a difference in public health issues ranging from child abuse to infants diagnosed with the human immunodeficiency virus (HIV). Yet she is the same doctor who was not allowed to add another two weeks to her four-week maternity leave to care for her twins, who were born prematurely and required extensive tube feeding.

Ellen Downing has become a master at ignoring the "Good Old Boys' Club" that persists in medicine and at her research center. "The group is very male. Women are cohesive as a group, but they don't run the show. I think when you're in a bureaucracy—and this is probably true in corporate America—advancement is very often more socially based than it is on productivity."

Both Ellen and her husband planned to get their careers well established, and in the same city, before they combined professions and parenthood. "My husband and I had been together for seven years before we had children. We moved around a lot; we received very good medical training, and we worked in good places.

"When we decided to have kids, it was done with the very conscious decision that, when we had them, they would become our highest priority—that nothing would come before them. There's a professional price to be paid for that commitment."

Like many other members of the "sandwich generation," Ellen has recently added another layer of responsibility: moving her mother, in her eighties, to California so that she can more

85

easily monitor her medical needs. For women trying to balance the needs of careers, children, and elderly parents, "Something's got to give," she says. "No one can do everything. I do have some career regrets, but my family is wonderful. As long as that is the case, I can live with the regrets."

MAKING A DIFFERENCE

Laura Tosi, MD, speaks with conviction of her deep concern for the social problems of the urban population she serves in Washington, D.C. "I see too many children themselves having children. And drug violence brings far too many teenage boys to our emergency room in critical condition. The hardest thing to learn is that you can't change the world."

Still, Laura tries to make a difference in people's lives as she helps to raise funds for disabled patients and specializes in care for children with birth defects. This is a woman with a clear mission.

People have to run to keep up with Laura Tosi as she passes through the swinging doors of the orthopedic ward. Her clear voice carries through the quiet halls as she confirms the final details of a 7:00 A.M. conference for her residents. Her precision and attention to detail are immediately apparent. "Is all the equipment here? How's the lighting? Is there coffee for everyone?"

Her daily hospital routine begins with 6:30 A.M. rounds and training of residents, before she launches into her "regular" day's work in the operating room. She carries a patient load of 80-100 a week, along with teaching surgery to young doctors. Hospital meetings late in the day mean that she cannot leave for home before 6:30 or 7:00 P.M.

With a schedule that is double that of the average workweek, what happens to her life at home?

Dinner preparations are timed to coincide with Laura's arrival at 7:30 P.M. She and her husband have managed to avoid the "erosive dinner conflict" that plagues so many two-career couples. They enjoy a relaxed dinner together each evening. The meal is prepared by their nanny, who has been with the family for nearly six years and, like Laura, works 12-hour days. Laura adds with a laugh, "We eat the leftovers from the week all weekend."

After dinner, Laura and her husband have time to play with the children. At 9:00 P.M., the children—and Laura—go to bed.

Laura's husband does all the grocery shopping, menu planning, and laundry, and has a major role in the children's care. "He came into this marriage committed to women's careers," she says. "I could not be me had I not had the extraordinary good fortune to meet this man."

She attributes her husband's willingness to assume "more than his fair share" of running their household to his own unusual upbringing. His mother is "much tougher, stronger, and more liberated than I will ever be." Laura tells the story of how her mother-in-law became an ardent feminist when, at age 32, she was forced to leave her teaching job because it was not considered proper for college students to see pregnant women.

Certain parts of Laura's schedule remain beyond her control. "One of the killer aspects of modern medicine is that we are buried alive by paperwork. I take home big bags of paperwork, which I do at 4:00 A.M. and for half a day each weekend." Every fourth night she is on call and may be up all night.

"Sometimes," she said quietly, "I must ask myself why I am doing this." Yet, she keeps going, trying to make a difference in the lives of the young patients she serves. Laura emphasizes: "The truth is, I love it. I love fixing things. Orthopedic surgery is the ultimate fixer-upper. It's a chance to make an immediate difference in the quality of someone's life. Few jobs provide that opportunity."

WHAT CAN WE LEARN FROM THE FAST-TRACKERS?

Few of us occupy corner offices in the executive suite or hold senior management positions among the Fortune 500. Even fewer can afford round-the-clock nannies. We can, however, learn valuable lessons from the women in this chapter, who have set clear goals and created well-defined visions for their lives. They also have stopped apologizing for their choices.

- **They do not feel guilty for their commitment to their jobs because they know they balance that commitment with devotion to their families.** Although they have broken through their professions' glass ceiling, all of the fast-trackers have made definite and carefully considered concessions in favor of family. Even the top wage earners know they would have climbed the career ladder faster and higher if they had not married or had children.

- **Even fast-trackers do not go it alone.** These women have supportive husbands and mentors; and, thanks to their high salaries, they can afford nannies. They also know that, in some cases, they had the good fortune to be in the right place at the right time. Because they carry a heavier load than their male counterparts, they rely on support and *real* help at home from their husbands. They say negotiation with their husbands is the key to the careful management that makes their lives run smoothly.

- **They are ultraefficient.** Fast-trackers are masters of management in the office and in the home: avoiding long commutes, arranging backup child care, catching up on paperwork when their children are asleep. Overachievers, they function regularly in overdrive. They set priorities with confidence and demonstrate grace under pressure.

- **They know they cannot keep up their high-speed pace without taking care of themselves.** Many fast-trackers use exercise as a buffer for the stress that comes with their territory. Some say their next goal is somehow to find the time for friendships, which often become the first sacrifice to a working mother's jam-packed schedule.

- **Most recommend establishing a career first.** A few of the fast-trackers we interviewed had started their families in their twenties. Most, however, had delayed childbearing until they were professionally secure. Virtually all the women in our survey said that they have been tested, by a boss or a peer, for wanting both profession and family. Those who waited to have children said that their senior positions gave them confidence that motherhood would not affect their professional ability. To get where they are today, they paid their dues with long hours, regular travel, and working on weekends early in their careers.

- **These women have spunk.** They want to come as close as humanly possible to having it all. If their professions place unfair and unnecessary obstacles in their path, they will switch jobs without regret. They *know* they can find success at the office and at home—and they refuse to crumble when criticized for trying to have both. All exhibit a strong sense of their own abilities and convey confidence in the office and in the home—thereby minimizing the inevitable role conflict between profession and family. Financial independence and career success play an important role in their overall sense of well-being and energize them to succeed in each of their roles.

- **They don't sweat the small stuff.** The fast-trackers have learned to concentrate on the big picture in each of their complex roles, and they have made themselves highly valued at work. They know they can still be good mothers even if they can't attend every Cub Scout meeting. They do, however, draw clear boundaries about when and if their professions begin to intrude on their closely guarded family time. Their self-confidence and their supportive husbands have enabled them to tune out negative judgments from others about how they are leading their lives.

- **They are determined to seek out jobs with companies that acknowledge family needs.** Some fast-trackers were willing to leave their jobs and find companies that accept people's commitment to the "hidden" side of their lives: their children. This courageous voting-with-your-feet lesson from the fast-trackers is our best hope for forging real change in the culture of work.

CHAPTER FOUR

◆ ◆ ◆

Tempering the Fast-Track:
Part-Time Careers

A three-day week; 9:00 A.M. to 3:00 P.M; job sharing. The personal advantages of a reduced work schedule are clear for women who want to spend more time with their children. Part-time work can mean a mother is available to attend afternoon school programs, greet her children when they get off the school bus, and take them to doctor's appointments.

We believed that part-time work, although still relatively untried, was *the* answer for many women caught in the work/family dilemma, that it was the best of both worlds. This was our hidden agenda as we began our research. However, the women we interviewed reminded us repeatedly that, from their own experience, part-time work is not yet the perfect answer.

Of course, not every job can be done part-time. Cardiovascular surgery and criminal law, for example, do not lend themselves to anything less than round-the-clock availability. We did find doctors who are job sharing or working reduced schedules on their own. A few MBAs have maintained their executive level while working part-time schedules. Some women have become law firm partners on a prorated basis, and their clients do not even know they are part-time.

Most part-timers are bargains for their organizations, working at peak efficiency and handling more than their fair share of the load. One of the few studies done on part-time productivity revealed that half-time social workers covered 89 percent of the caseload covered by full-timers.[1]

Part-time careers seemed the perfect bridge between commitment to career and immersion in family life, but we were caught off guard by the level of conflict and stress today's part-timers face:

• • •

A partner working 70-percent time in a Washington, D.C., law firm says, "I'm not going to be a major player at this law firm, and I'm not spending nearly as much time with my children as I'd like."

• • •

A New Hampshire attorney, working 32 hours a week, has regrets in each of her roles. "I'd be a partner now if I hadn't been on a part-time schedule. . . . I would prefer to be home after school with my kids, but I can't swing it financially."

• • •

A Washington State attorney who has worked 30 to 35 hours a week since her first child was born six years ago, reports: "It feels like the worst of all worlds—not enough time with the kids and not all that successful at work." Although she found it fairly easy to negotiate her contract of 20 billable hours a week, "Making it work is harder. It is very hard both to limit the time in the office and to meet work demands."

• • •

Deborah Maranville, a Seattle lawyer who has struggled with the work/family conflict, has similar feelings.

"While I like the idea of part-time, I think it's often difficult to do the most interesting work on a part-time basis. I also think there's some potential for the worst of all worlds—always feeling you should be working when you're with the kids, and vice versa."

• • •

A physician who works 25 to 30 hours as a hospital administrator says, "I still feel guilty on both counts. However, working half-time or less has made me feel half as guilty and provided a nice balance."

• • •

Many of the women who work part-time appear even more conflicted than the full-timers about the trade-offs between work and family. Did these women feel more torn from the start, or are they disappointed that going part-time results in so many professional trade-offs? What sets them up for this conflict and disappointment? What are the strategies women can use to apply the optimistic theory of part-time careers to achieve a successful reality?

OVERQUALIFIED AND UNDERPAID

Many employers view "part-time" and "professional" as mutually exclusive. Part-time professionals (women and men) constitute less than 3 percent of the work force.[2] Not enough women are working part-time to be able to assess reliably the merits. Nor are there enough data to forecast the long-term impact on a woman's career. However, the number of women working part-time demonstrates that women can be committed to their careers, valuable to their organizations, and practicing alternative work options—all at the same time.

There is no single definition of the term *part-time*. We encountered options ranging from five to 50 hours of work per week. Of the 902 Harvard Business, Law, and Medical school graduates who responded to our survey, one-third have held at least one part-time position since completing graduate school; 8 women reported that they have job shared, and 42 categorized themselves as having worked flextime. The part-time group ranged from a chief financial officer in a major corporation to a 6-hour-a-week doctor at a college health center.

Matina Horner, former president of Radcliffe College, has identified two levels for defining a profession: job and career.[3] Job means simply collecting a paycheck; career involves real commitment to and satisfaction derived from work. Some view their professions as a calling which denotes a nearly round-the-clock dedication and the ambition to function in high gear, regardless of personal costs. In theory, part-timers should be able to maintain a career, even if they must temporarily relinquish their ambition and drive for a calling.

A physician is still a doctor, whether she practices 5 hours a week or 75. A part-time attorney in a law firm may give up some of the "sexy" cases and pass up the opportunity for partnership, but maintain the prestige of a respected profession. For a woman with an MBA, however, the barriers are intimidatingly high to retaining professional respect and career momentum as a part-timer. This is the single overwhelming factor that forces many more MBA mothers to drop out than women in medicine and law, and explains why, of the three groups, MBAs are the least likely to be working part-time. Bosses and colleagues project a not-so-subtle skepticism about a part-timer's dedication to her profession, which undermines the high potential for rewarding and productive part-time careers.

Part-time work raises at least as many questions as it answers. Is it, as we originally thought, the best of both worlds? Or does it just place a career "on hold" in return for a less harried family life? How do clients and patients view part-time professionals? What happens to relationships with colleagues and bosses? What is the long-term career liability for a short-term slowing down? How are roles defined at home when one spouse has geared down at the office?

The work culture is generally unyielding in its lack of support for and promotion of part-time options. Women who work part-time challenge the most basic tenets of their professions: (1) You must make a choice between profession and family, (2) commitment can only be measured by time on the job, and (3) clients will not respect you unless you are available to them all the time. An article in the journal *MD*, on the barriers to women in medicine, cited the tightness of the male rules of the game, which are exclusionary to women who refuse to accept its tenets. In describing the informal grooming system for men in medicine, one male physician observed: "There was a prevailing attitude that women should not be doctors . . . because they were going to get married, have children, and work part-time. Medicine was seen by males as a kind of priesthood—and a part-time priesthood seemed unacceptable."[4]

Although not every part-timer loses ground professionally, today's unfortunate reality is that going part-time often derails a career. "Overqualified and underpaid" is the part-timers' refrain. The professional price for spending more time on parenting than on working can mean staying in a dead-end job, giving up a beloved specialty that involves unpredictable hours or heavy travel, or taking a disproportionately high cut in pay, with an even greater loss in professional respect and job security.

Part-timers are often disheartened by how much their professional egos suffer as they worry about the long-term impact on their careers. Yet they remain convinced that the extra time they gain with their children is still the best possible option for them—for now. Each of the following women presents a different slant on the uphill battle for rewarding part-time professional work. Each has made some inroads, and each points to strategies that can help make part-time careers a collective solution that really works.

A CAREER—NOT JUST A JOB

"If you go part-time, you're signaling to your employer you're on the B-team."[5]

The myth persists: The only way to be a professional is to work all the time. For those at the top, who set the tone for their organizations, work is the greatest source of personal reward. Time on the job is the premier measure of commitment. The myth also holds an added twist for the first full-fledged generation of women in the professions: There can be no compromise between the rewards of work and the value of family time; if you choose one, you will miss out on the other.

Alice Rogoff has a fax machine in her house, a phone in her car, and a beeper in her purse. Does this sound like someone who is uncommitted to her profession? Absolutely not. Alice is the chief financial officer (CFO) for a major U.S. media company—a position she maintains successfully as a part-timer.

Since her second child was born two years ago, Alice has worked a five-day schedule, 9:30 A.M. to 3:30 P.M., with no lunch break. Her arrangement is based on "unlimited availability" and immediate access from her home or car. What does she get in return? On most days, her schedule allows her to enjoy some of the most basic pleasures of parenting: greeting her daughter at the end of the school day, and having some time for everyone to unwind before beginning the family's dinner and bath routines.

Alice moves easily between her roles as mother and CFO, but says that combining career and family is a precarious balance. "It goes without saying that, whenever something compels me to stay at work in the afternoon, I stay at work, but it doesn't happen often."

Because she does not like to leave unfinished business, Alice uses some of her time at home after 3:30 P.M. to return phone calls or finish paperwork. She chose a reduced working day, rather than a shortened week, on purpose. "Even though I work shorter hours, I don't lose the tempo that I think you inevitably lose if you're not here every day. And I live close to the office—a 10-minute drive—so, if necessary, a messenger can bring things out to me."

Alice had worked for the company's president for three years before she broached the possibility of a reduced work schedule. "My boss has been very supportive from day one. We never put a time limit on my arrangement, but there are times when he jokes with me and says he would like me to *really* come back to work. My answer is that I *am* at work. I may not be physically there every minute, but work is never off my mind for one second."

She readily acknowledges her good fortune and the un-usual nature of her arrangement. "Another thing that makes this workable is that my boss is based in New York (I'm in Washington, D.C.), and so he deals with me by telephone anyway. I think that makes it easier for him not to be constantly annoyed at my not being nearby. If he were physically here, and I were not in the office, it would make it a lot harder."

Only one person in her company has resisted her part-time schedule: a young man, also a Harvard MBA, who has made clear his irritation when she leaves at 3:30 P.M. "I'm at a loss to explain his attitude," Alice says, "except that it's probably the dominant attitude in corporate America."

Alice supervises a staff of 40, including a growing number of part-timers, but she is the only executive working part-time. As good as her situation is, she has had to rein in her own ambition, because she knows "I have forfeited any chance to be a CEO [chief executive officer]—absolutely."

"In general," she says, "the corporate environment is too unforgiving of part-time work to be successful over the long haul. It is successful only for short-term intervals. Being CEO is a full-time job, and the reality is that I'm not going to return to full-time unless, God forbid, my husband were to vanish from the face of the earth and I couldn't afford not to."

How does it feel to give up the dream, fostered in part by intense training at the Harvard Business School, of becoming

CEO? For Alice Rogoff it has taken many years to say comfortably that she is willing to make the trade-off for the sake of her children. "At first I was unwilling to make it. I had only one child. But she got older, my second child was born and, over time, it's become much clearer to me that this is a choice I'm perfectly happy to make. Cutting back has clearly limited my professional advancement beyond where I am now, but after much ambivalence I am no longer unhappy with that limitation. In fact, I look forward to retiring from corporate life [in the not-for-profit sector] at some not-too-distant point."

Alice is beginning to think about how to reduce her hours further. "I get hit over the head from both my kids about why I'm not here, why I'm late, why I can't take them to school that day. Even though I'm home a lot, they want more."

Like many working mothers, Alice has discovered that her children may need her more, rather than less, as they get older. "It's a set of value judgments I make about parenting. I look around at working mothers who have delegated all of their child-raising to others—to nannies at best and, at worst, to housekeepers who don't speak English. And I don't like the results. It's not fair to the children. Once a child enters school, there's a lot a parent is expected to do—being around school, supervising lunch, going on field trips. It's all part of the experience for me."

ON THE B-TEAM

Sonia Becker,* MBA, has seen her image change from a high performer before her maternity leave to a member of the B-team—and not at all by choice. She is the only part-time professional employee at the large New York bank where she works 32 hours a week, down from the typical 45 or 50.

Choosing a reduced schedule is "not what people—co-

---

*An asterisk after a name designates a pseudonym.

workers, supervisors—expect from a dedicated employee. They want them available 24 hours a day," Sonia says. She could not convince her boss, also a working mother, that she could do her job part-time. However, her boss did support Sonia in finding another job at the bank.

Sonia strongly believes that her original job, which she dearly loved, could have been scaled down to part-time. She remains convinced that the real barrier was not her boss's concern about customer access, but her boss's prejudicial and unfounded assumptions about part-time.

"I think that after working part-time awhile you fall into this other category that people just don't think about much and don't consider as highly. My boss is a working mother who has handled her career very differently from mine. She is willing to delegate much of the child-rearing to her husband and babysitter in order to be very aggressive in her career."

Sonia cannot imagine spending 50 hours a week on her career and not seeing her children except on weekends. "That's just not my style," she says. However, she feels professionally vulnerable as a part-timer, particularly in a depressed economy. If people have to be let go, she thinks, the company will pick those employees who have been unwilling to prove their dedication by giving up most of their family time."

"I feel lonely and on my own with this," Sonia says. "It's difficult to complain when I look at this objectively. I'm in an enviable position. I have a husband who is working. I have two wonderful children. I have a job that is interesting. And yet I feel this malaise. I don't feel I'm entirely dedicated at work, and I don't feel I'm spending quality time at home, either."

DETOUR FROM TRADITION

Renee Matalon has developed a career that is nontraditional for a Harvard Law School graduate, but she fulfills her personal values and meets the priorities she has set as a parent. She works four days a week as an attorney for the Agency for International Development (AID). Her objective for this job: "It had to be sane."

Renee has never quite felt that she fit as a lawyer, despite her traditional training. "I am disturbed about how work obsessed the law culture is. The expected billable hours go up by 200 to 400 hours every year: about 1,600 in 1981; in 1983, about 1,800; now 2,000 to 2,200 is more common."

Renee's career took a detour from corporate law when she worked as editor of *Washington Jewish Week* before landing her current job at AID. Renee was not yet pregnant when she took this job, but she specifically sought a position that would not require evening and weekend work. During the employment interview, she asked pointed questions about the agency's work ethic: What are your work hours? What are your expectations for your lawyers? What do people do outside of work? Do they have personal interests other than their jobs?

The common culture at AID focuses on commitment to Third World countries rather than on a specific work style to meet the agency's goals. Some employees work long hours; others do not. Because many of the staff travel to developing countries for long periods, few people notice Renee's absence one day a week. Even when she took a four-month maternity leave her boss was comfortable approving her time away because he was accustomed to people disappearing for a few months at a time. Also, Renee knew, through her interview, that he, too, took seriously making time for his family life.

Renee sometimes feels caught between two worlds. "I feel kind of lonely. Out of our 35 lawyers, only two women have children, and one is in Asia now." Renee has not met any other women who are working part-time. The women who have dropped out seem to have put aside their professional identities and want to talk only about their children. The mothers she meets at her son's nursery school, who have never worked outside the home, seem to question her commitment to motherhood.

In her current job, Renee cannot do "the fun stuff in the field" because she and her family would not move overseas, which is where the action is. Although she is slowing her career, she feels an intense need to find her "calling" when her children are older. "I have high expectations for what I want to accomplish with my life. I need to do something that will have a real impact on the world." She knows for certain, however, that she will never return to a traditional law practice, where she "always felt she had landed on the wrong planet." For now, "my priority is the mothering part, and there will be time to explore other things down the road."

PURSUING THEIR CALLING

A small number of part-timers in our survey have come close to pursuing their calling. Being in the right place at the right time is often the key to their success.

Ten years ago, the possibility that a department chair of cardiology would be both female and part-time would have been unheard of. Even for Dr. Joan Haskell, who holds this position at a Maryland hospital, it took two serious attempts before she got what she wanted.

After her first child was born, Joan reduced her hours at another hospital from 80 to between 45 and 60 a week. Despite this grueling version of "part-time," and praise from the hospital director for her four years of full-time work, Joan was told that she would never become a member of the corporation. She would have to sacrifice even prorated bonuses and could not participate in department decisions or serve on hospital committees.

The irony was that she was expected to assume full-time on-call duty and cover all holidays, along with the one other

101

part-timer in the group. Despite her dramatically reduced pay, Joan continued to deal with 90 percent of the average patient load for full-timers.

As discouraged as she was for having to "grovel" for part-time status, Joan was not surprised at her colleagues' attitude. These were the same people who would not allow her sick leave to take her toddler for chemotherapy. Their reaction to her request for part-time work was all too easy to predict.

Her story, however, has a happy ending. Joan now works three days a week as chief cardiologist for a small hospital. Although she does not see the range of challenging cases that she saw in her former position, she has negotiated a fair, pro-rated salary and has two full days each week to spend with her two young children. She is treated with respect at her new reduced-schedule job, where "I thought I had arrived in paradise."

ACT LIKE A PARTNER

The old adage "Law is a jealous mistress" can hit women with particular fury. Conventional wisdom says that women attorneys should make partner before having children, mainly because of the virtually inviolable seven-year, up-or-out law firm standard. The rules for the seven-year trial are generally unyielding: Demonstrate commitment by working long hours every day, and make sure you come into the office most weekends. How can dedication like this possibly be tempered to accommodate part-time lawyers?

An article in the *Stanford Lawyer* referred to female lawyers as an "endangered species" and reported: "Women are leaving law firms in record numbers. New, more flexible policies could stop the brain drain."[6] Lawyers have traditionally assumed that they cannot become a partner if they work part-time. However, we discovered women who have challenged that assumption.

Part-time attorney Lynn Hart says, "I am a partner in my

firm, run my department, and do extensive professional speaking. In addition, I can participate in my children's lives. I can do a toddler program with our youngest, drive the car pool, and be a presence at home. It is *not* effortless, or even easy, but it works (most of the time!)."

Lynn works 60-percent time, about 30 hours a week, for 50-percent pay. It took an extra year for her to make partner. Although her legal expertise certainly played a major role in her career success, working part-time also depended on planning and timing.

Lynn took a careful look at legal specialties during the year she clerked for a judge and another year she worked at a corporate litigation firm. "I looked around at the people more senior than I was. I didn't see life-styles I wanted to emulate—with or without a family. I wanted more balance in my life." Lynn counts herself fortunate to have found part-time work in estate-planning law, which she enjoys. She also appreciates that her specialty includes fewer emergencies and generally gives her control over her deadlines, an important secret to success as a part-timer.

While pregnant with her first child, Lynn was offered a position as an associate with the law firm. "There's something you should know," she told them. "I'm three months pregnant. I want to take six months off for maternity leave and then work no more than 60-percent time." Not surprisingly, their answer was, "We'll call you back." And they did. Though the partners admitted they didn't know how to react to her proposal, they agreed to talk further.

Lynn's delicate negotiations took place during the week that the 50-person firm was about to vote on a part-time policy that would explicitly preclude part-timers from becoming partners. Lynn was hired for a 60-percent load by a full-firm vote—with the understanding that she would still be considered for partnership. At the time, there was not yet enough work in estate planning to support a full-time associate. As Lynn describes it, "We met on the margin with 60 percent."

Lynn used her maternity leave to reconsider her goals for professional achievement. "For me, 'success' would be the ability to continue to work part-time." She knew that clients and colleagues would be skeptical. "My assumption was that my ability to do this would depend on the comfort levels of those I work with. The key to that comfort level would be availability. Their fear was that I would not be there when they needed me."

Lynn's schedule is unusual, but it works well. She comes into the office full days on Mondays and Fridays, and works afternoons on Tuesdays and Thursdays. She scheduled half days for the afternoons because many lawyers spend their mornings in court or in meetings. Coming in later in the day is less intrusive to the law firm work ethic than making the rather visible statement of leaving before 6 P.M.

She gives her home phone number to certain clients who may need to call her on a Wednesday, but finds that most clients can forego a day of her attention midweek. "There are times when it gets intrusive; but, again, one of the issues for me was accessibility."

Lynn maintains some of the traditional aspects of being a lawyer. She supervises an all-female team of two part-time lawyers, two part-time legal assistants, and two full-time secretaries, and credits the group with knowing when to fill in for her and when to call her at home. She sets aside every Tuesday night for her work overflow, while her husband Fred, a corporate securities lawyer, takes care of their children.

On the home front Lynn describes herself as the shock and stress absorber. "I tend to be the one who takes the bumps in the road. My husband is very supportive and very involved with the children, but he is clearly the primary wage earner. His salary is more than double mine. For me to be home with the children is the role that I want. Every once in a while Fred suggests that he stay home and I work full-time." She adds with a laugh, "I just glare at him."

Lynn is facing a crossroads now that she is expecting her third child. How will the baby change the balance she has achieved between work and home? Thus far there have been no trade-offs. She is the only part-time partner in her firm and commands wide respect for her writing and public speaking. Every other year she further reduces her work load to teach a course in estate planning at Stanford Law School.

The time for making a major career sacrifice may be coming soon for Lynn Hart. She would like to reduce her part-time schedule to 40 or 50 percent, but is quite certain that such a reduction would mean giving up her partnership. She has not decided what to do. She knows that she has been accepted by her firm, but she is still considered the exception. "In most cases you need to make 100 percent commitment—that's *the* buzzword—to make it work at one of these firms."

"THE TONE COMES FROM THE TOP"

Sharon Tisher is one of two part-time partners in a 79-partner law firm in Hartford, Connecticut. She is proud of her firm and feels good about her role. "We are the only law firm of our size and caliber that has two part-time partners, one of whom never worked full-time."

Sharon was made partner after five years of full-time work at the law firm and 2½ years of a reduced work load of 80 percent after the birth of her first child. Her part-time status does not rule out cases that require her to be at work 100 percent of the time. "When I am on trial, I'm a lawyer 100 percent. I think that's a very positive and realistic way to practice. I travel when necessary and work evenings as required." When she took on a two-month trial in Boston, Sharon commuted home only on the weekends, while her husband cared for their two children during the week.

The normal routine for Sharon and her husband is for each

to work a four-day week, with each having a different day at home. Each saves commuting time and, if one of the children gets sick, they have more flexibility. Sharon has day-care coverage for every day of the week, so she chooses her day at home according to what is most convenient for her work load. She is in the office four days a week, from 9:00 A.M. to 5:00 P.M., and generally works after her children are asleep. She is a full-equity partner in the firm and receives 80 percent of the partnership distribution that a partner at her level of seniority would otherwise receive. If she were full-time, she would need to be in the office until at least 7:00 P.M. each evening.

Most part-time arrangements still happen on an ad hoc basis. In Sharon Tisher's case, the firm already had a policy for maternity leaves and part-time work, written by a committee of women at the firm.

Sharon believes that "the tone comes from the top" and credits her firm with her 80 percent arrangement. "They realize that half of the work force now coming out of law school are women who . . . often . . . want a more flexible work schedule. And I think they perceive it as equitable and reasonable not to deprive these women of partnership."

TEMPERING EXPECTATIONS

From outward appearances, Liz Nill has it made. Comfortably dressed in a skirt and sweater, she greeted us in her small office at Harvard's Kennedy School of Government. An MBA, class of 1979, Liz was assistant dean at the Harvard Business School for five years, took a 10-week maternity leave, then returned to her 50-hour-a-week job. Within a year, she had "hit the wall."

"I nearly broke down that year," Liz says. "I was exhausted—running to the [on-site] day-care center every two hours to nurse [her baby]. I had this image of myself as a supermother, that I could do it all—work, be on boards, cook the meals, renovate the house."

Finally, she faced her limits. "I remember, I came home and put my daughter to bed, and then I collapsed on the couch and said to my husband, 'I can't do this anymore. I just can't do it.' I didn't know whether to stop working [or] find a part-time job. It was pretty much of a crisis, and I wasn't happy with my daughter being in a day-care center all day. It was too much."

Liz seriously considered dropping out of the work force entirely, but finally concluded that "I couldn't stop working. The idea of not working at all was terrifying. The prospect of receiving my total intellectual and emotional stimulation from my immediate family was daunting."

She now works 25 to 30 hours a week, directing a program for cabinet-level state officials at the Kennedy School. (In July she works nearly around the clock.) When she accepted the job, it was full-time. "It was a delicate, interesting series of negotiations," Liz says, "and the dean was generous enough to let me convince him that part-time would work." Trade-offs were part of the deal, mainly in salary, "but the school was getting someone overqualified and underpaid." She negotiated no travel initially, but now that her children are older she accepts some job-related trips.

Liz loves the job she has held for six years, although it is not precisely on her career track (she wants to be a college president). "It's visible, very sexy, on the cutting edge," she says. When her second child was born three years ago, she found it much less traumatic to return to work. "I don't think you can have two intensely career-driven people and have a family unit. One person in the family has to be willing to assume a supportive role. In my case, it happens to be me. I love being a mother. I also love working. Both give me a role in society. And when I'm tempted by other jobs that would take more time, I remind myself that I had these children and

I have a responsibility. I just can't walk out on them for something that would give *me* more satisfaction."

Liz Nill advises others seemingly caught in the no-woman's-land between profession and family: "Don't expect too much of yourself, nor give away too much. You have to let go of something." She is clear that she has relinquished some of her professional ambition—in all likelihood, only for the short term.

REINING IN AMBITION

People who know that Ruth Payson* has an MBA from Harvard seem puzzled that she is "not running and gunning, ready to eat up the world, hard charging, hard driving." They thought she was going to be the stereotypical MBA—and she wasn't.

Ruth's first nontraditional MBA move was to locate in Portland, Maine, which she and her husband knew would be a great place to rear children. Her second decision, which surprised even her, was to move off the management track as soon as her daughter was born. She is now a training consultant for an insurance company in Maine.

"I wouldn't say I've terminated all chances of my ever progressing, but I am doing something now I'm sure I would not be doing if I had continued full-time for the last eight years. I'm at the same level that I was when I went part-time. With all due humility, I am sure I would be further along if I had devoted myself to a full-time career."

Ruth, a mother of two children, aged four and eight, began her career at the company as manager of a small products line. When she moved to her three-day-a-week job in training and development, she lost her disability coverage, her personal days, and participation in the company's matching gift program. "It's just sort of a pervasive atmosphere. It's as if your part-time job is a hobby, that you're not interested in a career, that you're not serious about it."

Having a child changed her, Ruth says. "I thought I would be back after six weeks. My boss at the time had two kids of his own and said, 'You may change your mind. Feel free to change your options after the baby is born.' I did have a change of heart. I ended up taking 4½ months off." However, Ruth wanted to come back to work. "I thought I'd go nuts at home all the time. On the other hand, I wanted to spend time with my baby. I realized I didn't want to go back to traveling and be away 30 percent of the time."

After her maternity leave, Ruth left her management position and negotiated a part-time position with the vice-president of her division. At first, she worked two days a week on special projects. After a year, she moved up to three days a week and is now paid for 25 hours a week, but generally ends up working about 35 hours—and is still considered part-time. She is in the office on Tuesdays, Wednesdays, and Thursdays and works at home other mornings and on weekends. Because many of her clients are on the West Coast, she does a lot of her phone work from home in the evenings.

Most of Ruth's clients are themselves on the road and have no concerns about how many hours she is physically in the company's office. "I answer calls as frequently as my full-time counterparts—from wherever I am." However, over the years she has not found other supervisors as supportive as the vice-president who first let her work part-time. "It's not out of maliciousness, but from a basic lack of open-mindedness."

Regardless of their professional level, part-timers worry about job security. For some, the arrangement fully depends on a particular boss. Ruth Payson almost lost her job during a recent downsizing that looked at head count, rather than full-time equivalents. The result was that all other part-timers were laid off. Ruth was saved only because no one else was trained to do her work. Of 4,000 company employees, only 2 professionals work part-time. "They make a big deal out of having on-site day care and say they promote a work/home balance," Ruth says, "yet they don't offer any substantive benefits to part-timers. My company talks a good game, but their actual policies do not support alternative work situations. The culture is anti-part-time."

THE DOWN SIDE

Dr. Jill Stein's story illustrates many of the disadvantages of part-time work—difficult to find for professional women, and if available at all, at the cost of job security, benefits, and accrued seniority.

"Initially, I worked very hard and incurred much family- and child-related stress in order to be the reliable doctor/employee," Jill says. "It took me 10 years to learn that I could interrupt my career to have a better family life. Now that I know that, I consider it a successful combination. I look forward to returning to a more intensive career when my family life allows it." Because of the 80 hours a week that her husband works in his medical specialty, Jill describes herself as a "functionally single parent."

Jill recently accepted her most part-time job ever: six hours a week at a college health center in Boston. Relaxed in a warm-up suit, with her golden retriever at her feet, she reflects, "I'm glad to be relinquishing my career to be more of a parent. I find parenting infinitely more complex, challenging, and rewarding than medicine."

When she had her first child, Jill was working 30 hours a week at a health maintenance organization (HMO) and commuting two hours a day to one of the few part-time positions in the area. When her second child was born, Jill realized "it doesn't have to be this constant tug of war. Whose needs are going to take priority? I thought, my God, being a parent can be fun. I decided not to go back to work at all."

After six months at home, Jill received a call from a health maintenance organization, saying they were desperate for internists. "I could come in whatever hours I wanted—8 to 12 hours a week—no evenings, no weekends. It was irresistible."

Indeed, the job proved a bit too good to be true. "Initially, I wasn't going to do rounds. Then I said 'OK' and started doing rounds on the days I worked. Then they wanted me to do rounds even on the days I didn't have appointments."

Five years into her job, Jill faced a new set of choices. The HMO was ready to reduce its employee head count, and Jill would have to work at least 25 hours a week, plus do rounds, to remain a permanent staff member. She decided instead to give her notice and look for "real" part-time work. It wasn't easy. She found few opportunities for half-time physicians (defined usually as 25 to 30 hours a week).

Jill Stein knows definitely that she has "minimized" her career, but says she has no regrets. "My missed achievements feel very shallow and transient to me compared with the fulfillment of parenthood." In the past, she has encountered some resentment from her colleagues for her part-time status—when they forgot that she is paid much less than they are. She also reached the same conclusions we heard from many other physicians: "Medicine just doesn't have the rewards it used to have."

Jill *is* leaving the door open for a second career in medicine by practicing at least enough to keep her skills and references current. She regrets that her generation has few mentors to demonstrate that women can return to professional careers even after long parenting sabbaticals. Yet she also feels optimistic about figuring out how to do it. Even in medicine, she says, it *is* possible to come back after 15 years. Success, however, depends on learning "many tricks of the trade" for remaining current and visible in a specialty and assuring that people continue to think of you as a professional.

IS PART-TIME THE ANSWER?

Emily Perkins,* an attorney, is in conflict over the work/family dilemma: Is her career rewarding enough to warrant missing out on time with her child?

111

"I have one of the best part-time arrangements I know of, and am the envy of many other working (and nonworking) mothers, but I still often think of quitting to stay home with my daughter, and I feel this more as she gets older.

"I often feel that, by combining both [career and motherhood], I'm neither a good lawyer nor a good mother. Also, I feel guilty about working, since we could scrape by without my salary, but I feel that working, especially where I'm able to complete a task, improves my self-esteem."

Emily points out how negative perceptions about the part-time concept diminish the potential rewards from having the best of both worlds. "The male and female partners for whom I work are equally supportive in theory. [They are] nonsupportive in practice when my part-time schedule means I do less work than others, or need more time to complete work."

Emily works in health care law three days a week, 10:00 A.M. to 4:00 P.M. She has paid a price for this flexibility: changing her specialty from ERISA [Employment Retirement Income Security Act] pension work to health care law, which involves no discovery or lengthy depositions. "It's difficult to litigate part-time. You quickly lose control of your schedule. Everything is a crisis."

Before she married, Emily was on the partnership track, with impressive credentials from an Ivy League college and Harvard Law School. She worked every night and never hesitated to change personal plans for the sake of her work. In the beginning, her career seemed patterned after the traditional law school fast track: first a position in the federal government, then a job with a large, prestigious Washington, D.C., law firm.

When she became a mother, however, she began to wonder whether "success" in the workplace was enough to compensate for the 60-plus hours each week that kept her away from her family and forced her to be a weekend parent.

Her excellent track record as a part-timer at another firm

opened the door to negotiating with her current firm. "This went against all conventional wisdom that says that only a present employer will give you part-time." In fact, she made the firm an offer they could not refuse: she would be paid by the hour, receive no benefits, and would take herself off the partnership track.

Emily also discovered that part-timers can promote themselves to small firms, which tend to be top-heavy with partners. Small firms have neither the time nor the money to invest in training associates fresh from law school. Seasoned part-timers, who don't need training, look pretty good to them, she says.

Emily is proud to be a trailblazer for a nontraditional law practice. "I was the first part-time lawyer at my firm and had to persuade the partners it would work. After eight months, the firm hired another female attorney on the same part-time schedule as mine, so the partners clearly believe the arrangement is in the firm's interests."

Most of Emily's clients do not even know that she is part-time. Long-term clients do know and are sympathetic, she says. Emily plays down her nontraditional status, not because of her own clients but because "I'm concerned that adversaries would not take me seriously if *they* knew."

Fundamental trade-offs come from placing limits on your time at work. For Emily, this means refusing the most challenging cases if she knows they will not fit into her three-day work schedule.

Emily characterizes herself as "ruthlessly efficient." "I think the firm has a good deal with me, since I spend less time hanging out [and] gossiping at the office than do full-time associates. I also picked a less high-pressure, small firm, where my skills as a lawyer are in high demand (in contrast to my prior firm—a high-profile 'boutique' with lots of superstars and superegos). My part-time arrangement works because I've made myself indispensable."

IT'S MURKY AT THE TOP

The higher the job level, the less clear the definition of part-time work becomes. Dana Powers* considers the 30 hours she works as a government attorney "part-time," but says her status is unclear to her employer and her colleagues. She also has noticed that the part-time work policies put on the books under President Jimmy Carter fell by the wayside in actual practice under the administrations of Ronald Reagan and George Bush. Part-time work still exists, of course, but Dana sees it happening only on an ad hoc, case-by-case basis for women with solid full-time track records.

"It's a murky picture," Dana says. "Some people [at the office] don't even know I work part-time. Those who do make jokes about my easy life. They think I'm coasting and that I'm really supposed to be working 40 hours a week." Although she is paid for 24 hours a week, she consistently puts in between 30 and 35 hours because "no one is clear how it's supposed to work. I work as many hours as it takes to get the job done. I'm usually in Monday through Thursday, 9 to 6, and off on Friday."

Dana is very conscious of pulling her proportionate weight with the full-timers. "I do get paid for all the hours I work up to 40 hours. I have the sense that people who get paid for 40 hours are expected to be putting in more hours, so I don't put down all the hours I work above the 24 in my contract."

Dana knows that a reduced workweek and paycheck do not trigger a reduction in necessary tasks at home, and she says that her live-in help is essential to her survival. "My housekeeper runs my house, grocery shops, cooks, takes the two kids to school, picks them up." Dana realizes she is fortunate to be able to afford household help that allows her to expand her office hours whenever her work demands. Unlike some part-timers, Dana does not place strict limits on her work load. Yet, her part-time status means that she is not doing precisely what she set out to do—although she comes close.

Dana set the tone for her flexibility by accommodating her employer's needs during her first maternity leave. Although she had requested and been approved for a four-month leave, she returned after six weeks to argue a case she had been working on before the birth of her child.

"I had no child care arranged for me, and no one, including my husband, could help me out on the morning I had to go to court. So I took an associate from the office, an expectant father, to help me take my new baby to court. I placed the baby between us, and he fell asleep for two hours."

Three months into her leave, Dana was asked to come to court to back up another attorney. "My office knew then that I was a committed professional. From then on, for the rest of my leave, I was in one day a week, often with my baby." People at work noticed her professional dedication. "When I came back for 'real' and said I wanted to work part-time, they were predisposed to say 'all right.' They realized, 'This person has been with us for seven years, and we can count on her in a crunch. And she's gotten great performance ratings.' "

The highest toll for part-timers is loss of professional respect, Dana says. "I used to do the emergency work—restraining orders and preliminary injunctions. It was very exciting—quick and dirty." She used to travel all over the country on major cases, often for a month at a time. These are the cases she turns down now.

"I've cut back my work dramatically and stay in a dead-end job to make the time to have kids. I don't know anybody who has a combination that is without its stresses and strains," she adds, but, for her, going part-time was and remains the best choice. "My children have enriched me immeasurably and were worth everything I had to give up."

PRICE TAG FOR PART-TIME

There are two ways to work part-time, each of which comes with a price. Some part-timers set limits on the hours they work. While they gain "clean," well-defined family time, they often lose professional status and essentially place their careers in a holding pattern. Others, like Dana Powers and CFO Alice Rogoff, are always "on call" because of the level of their positions. Their nearly unlimited availability to their employer means their time at home is never really their own.

Part-time work continues to be slanted in favor of employers; generally it remains a very good business deal for the boss. Potential exists, however, for employers and part-timers to create a more balanced partnership—if each side is willing.

When a woman chooses to work less than full-time, she is not saying that she is throwing away all her hard-earned professional training. Instead, she is refusing to give up either of the two important parts of her life. She wants to keep her salary, her self-image, and her professional success—all part of the career pull traditionally reserved for men. Yet she also wants the flexibility to attend her child's soccer game, bake brownies for the PTA, and take her child to the dentist—simple parenting tasks whose meaning is important to her. She has come to realize that "quality time" is not enough, either for herself or her children. She can thrive part-time in her career if she and her employer can reach a reasonable and fair arrangement.

Although many women in part-time jobs feel frustrated by or resigned to their stalled careers, their professional situations are temporary. Over time, their lives may well prove to be more gratifying because of the choices they have made for family and for work, and for ultimately experiencing the best from both worlds.

MAKING THE DECISION

The success of part-time work essentially hinges on three elements:

1. **Definition.** How part-time can you be in your profession? What is a realistic schedule for meeting the needs of your boss and your clients? How much work do you plan to bring home?

2. **Accessibility.** What kind of limits will you set on the boundaries between work and home? Can you be available for crisis situations?

3. **Visibility.** How will you deal with perceptions about professional commitment when your schedule is different from the rest of your colleagues? Can you employ technology to make your work visible even when you are not in the office?

To help you decide if part-time work is the answer for you, consider the following key questions:

- Can you scale down your full-time work to part-time, or can some of your responsibilities be reassigned to someone else?

- Are there other jobs in which you could be a valuable contributor on a part-time basis?

- Are you willing to continue to travel, to work evenings, to work weekends?

- Do you want to be paid for actual hours worked or on a flat salary?

- Can you be accessible when you are not in your office— by telephone, by messenger, by fax?

- Would you prefer a set schedule that establishes a clean break between work and home?

- Can you afford to earn less if you have established a life-style that depends on two full-time incomes? Will your job become less secure if you go part-time?

- Can you and your family do without some of the bene-fits and extra compensation that you will lose when you reduce your hours?

- Will you be able to arrange flexible part-time child care? Part-time work sometimes requires give-and-take be-tween your hours at home and at the office. For exam-ple, you may be asked or expected to attend important meetings on your day off. Can your child-care arrange-ments cover such contingencies?

- Are you going to set limits on your availability and stick to those limits, or will you be totally accessible? Each option holds distinct personal and professional advan-tages and disadvantages.

Following are suggestions for negotiating your part-time arrangement from a position of strength:

- **Make yourself indispensable to your organization by establishing an outstanding track record.** If your boss really needs your talents, it will be harder to refuse you part-time work.

- **Negotiate with a well thought-out plan in hand.** An-ticipate your employer's concerns and present workable solutions. Offer a review period for your part-time ar-rangement, during which your new status will be pro-bationary. Make it impossible to turn you down.

118

- **Consider whether it is really necessary to tell clients or patients that you are working part-time.** If they do not need to know, perhaps there is no need to tell them.

- **Avoid long commutes.** A long drive to and from the office eats into your part-time workday and reduces your overall flexibility.

- **Don't apologize for your choice.** Recognize that your self-esteem may take a temporary drop when you decide to temper your professional ambition. Balance the loss by focusing on the personal rewards you will see on the home front and on the long-term goals you have set for your family and career.

- **Plan far in advance—even before you have children—if you think you might ever want to work part-time.** How does your profession and its work environment mesh with your future plans? A part-time law partner suggests, "If your age permits, get settled into a job that you plan to keep, become indispensable, and gain a reputation for hard work. Then have children."

CHAPTER FIVE

◆ ◆ ◆

Off the Beaten Path: The New Entrepreneurs

Pat Jacobs, a divorced mother of three, founded K-Com, a consulting firm in management information systems, eight years ago. She says she likes being an entrepreneur. "I tell the tale that, although every day I come in to the office and get my butt kicked, I go home, grin, and come in the next day and get kicked some more."

"I probably like the challenge, and clearly enjoy the flexibility of being my own boss—and the financial rewards, albeit apparently delayed," Pat said with a wry smile.

This high-spirited woman chose children, single motherhood, and her own business over a traditionally structured, higher paying job. She works 12-hour days and earns less than she did as an attorney, but Pat has enough control over her schedule to ease the pressure of single parenting. She employs a highly skilled, live-in nanny, but says there are many aspects of parenting that she does not want to delegate to someone else.

"When we finish this interview, I'm going to take my children to their doctor's appointment," she said from her Washington, D.C., office. "I can certainly take time off to go to my child's school during the day. There's not the issue that I'm going to ruin my career by doing that."

Pat Jacobs is a classic example of the new breed of entrepreneur: women who have chosen to leave the traditional, rigid corporate structure for a chance to become their own bosses. She and many other women we surveyed are pursuing a new and powerful agenda: they want to succeed in their work, but on their own terms.

For many of these women, the catalyst for self-employment was a life crisis rather than a passionate urge to open a new lemonade stand.

Pat Jacobs became an entrepreneur quite by accident. Her other options simply would not work for her family: a six-year-old child from her marriage, and two newly adopted babies, seven months and eight months old.

She had worked on Capitol Hill as counsel to a Senate business committee, then ran a trade association for venture capital investors. Eight years ago, she had enough money put aside to buy the assets of a small company that had gone out of business and to start her own firm. Today she has a staff of 40 employees.

"The story I always tell is that I was making lots of speeches around the country about being in business, and I met all these people who are entrepreneurs," Pat said. "They were *always* smiling. I didn't know at the time that there was a fine line between lunacy and happiness. I thought they were happy!"

As her own boss, Pat feels no guilt when she leaves work to attend daytime school events or needs to be away from the office to be with her children when they are ill. True, there are weekends when she has to work, but she thrives on running her own show and still has enough energy at the end of the day to enjoy the time she spends with her children.

Like most Harvard Law School graduates, Pat has moments when she measures her own success by traditional male yardsticks. "This is not easy, running a business. I always read these Harvard surveys about how much everyone is making, and I don't make half that much," she said. "It would be very easy to go back into law, but that is precluded by my need for flexibility—for my children and for my life-style." Over the long-term, Pat's earning potential may well prove higher than if she had remained in the traditional work culture, where women earn 70 cents for every dollar a man brings home.[1]

PROFILE OF THE NEW ENTREPRENEUR

Among the 902 women we surveyed, nearly 30 percent are now or, at some point in their careers, have been self-employed. Women now outnumber men three to one in the start-up of their own companies, most of which are relatively small and often home-based.[2] "Add in the part-time enterprises operated out of homes, and about 70 percent of the new businesses founded in the U.S. last year were owned by women," according to a recent *Fortune* article.[3] The National Foundation for Women Business Owners projects that in the next year women-owned businesses will outpace Fortune 500 companies in the number of new job openings.[4]

Like men who go it alone, these women are looking for professional autonomy, but they differ in their search for control not only over *what* they do but over *how* they do it. A recent cover story in *Fortune*[5] referred to entrepreneurs as "dropouts," because they had chosen to let go of the traditional and, at times, unreasonable standards of corporate behavior: unnecessary and unproductive meetings; spur-of-the-moment travel assignments; bosses who could not have cared less if their employees had personal lives.

For women who want family lives as well as careers, those images paint a grim picture. The corporate "dropouts" we met had lost faith in the professions to which they had given their souls. They no longer were willing to accept the degree of personal sacrifice associated with traditional success. The stereotype of the entrepreneur with the massive ego—expansive enough to conquer impossible odds—does not hold for the women we met. Many have consciously chosen instead to hold their professional ambition in check for the sake of family time—and yet they are still, by anyone's standards, running rewarding and profitable businesses.

In one key way, the women we surveyed also reflect the spirit of the classic (usually male) entrepreneurs portrayed in business textbooks. They are willing to take calculated risks to try to create what they want: an organization that reflects their personal values. Unlike most of the risk-takers who had come before them, however, the women we surveyed have built a real partnership between work and family. Their goal: greater satisfaction and self-esteem by creating more balanced lives that they can control themselves.

That is the basic package; but, in the true entrepreneurial spirit, each of the women we surveyed has brought her own approach to finding the balance that works for her career, her family situation, and her children. Few say they have all the flexibility they would like in their jobs—but they are close, much closer than if they had stayed in traditional corporate structures.

They also are realistic about how well they have done in balancing careers and children. Some needed more than one try to make self-employment work, but they say the effort has been worth it. The glory for these women does not lie in how high their tax bracket soars but in how successful they can become *and* still enjoy their families.

The new entrepreneurs have accepted that they must ease up a bit on what they expect from each part of their lives. Maybe this is why these women, as a group, seem more at peace with their lives—hectic as their schedules might be— than they might have been had they made other life-style choices.

The content of their professional work had been fine before they struck out on their own. The context of that life was the problem. What was missing was control over *when* the work got done. Most of the women said that they had no problem working in groups or as part of a team, but they became frustrated by corporate team rules based on the theory that there is only one way to get a job done. They made a bold choice: to create businesses of their own that reflected values decidedly absent in the rigid work culture. And the odds are in their favor that they *will* succeed. The National Federation of Independent Business uncovered the good news that 77 percent of new companies founded since the mid-1980s are still in operation at least three years later—this quite contrary to the traditional pattern of three of five new ventures going belly-up in their early years.[6]

In this chapter, we will present portraits of some of the risk-takers who have dared to leave the traditional career track and follow their own paths. As a group, they shared these traits:

- Most continue to work more than 40 hours a week.

- All say they have never considered dropping out of the work force entirely.

- Most do not earn as much as they did during their corporate careers, regardless of how long they have been self-employed.

- Balance, between career and family, is their most powerful motivation for risk.

- Their professional goals are based on autonomy and flexibility.

- They say there is no question but that family comes first.

- They know how to divide their personal and professional lives into "compartments," and to set limits at home and at work.

- They are determined to create a work culture that has room for professional success *and* a sane life-style. Most are driven by balance rather than by ambition; by stable self-employment rather than by fame and fortune.

- They know they cannot afford to be loners. Behind every strong entrepreneur is strong support, perhaps a husband who acts as the primary parent, or a compatible business partner with shared values for both work and home.

- Most say they will never "go back" unless they do not have a choice.

WORKING FOR YOURSELF

Lawyer Alice Ballard has tough, practical advice for women who want to direct their own professional lives. "Force yourself to save 50 percent of your pay," she tells new law school graduates starting out in big firms. "Restrict your living standard, if necessary. Do that for a few years while you learn to be a lawyer. Then you will be free to go into self-employment—the only real way to control your career."

In 1976 Alice and a partner founded their own Philadelphia law practice, specializing in employment law and industrial accidents. For the next four years, before she was married and had children, Alice worked 80 hours a week, building her professional reputation. After her marriage, she decided to work a 9-to-6 business day. Now the mother of two young children, ages one and five, Alice works 3½ days a week.

Alice plans to ease back into a 4½-day week soon but, in the meantime, she tells the world she is working full-time, and no one knows the difference.

"There is too much stigma associated with 'part-time' in the practice of law," she said. "I think that law firms are trying to give people flexibility but, in fact, the best they can do is to take people from 80 hours to 40 hours. If you want to go to your kid's school play and be there when you please, you pretty much have to work for yourself."

Alice has done a good job of setting limits on a professional work load that could easily overflow into the time she has at home with her children. When clients call her at home, she tells them directly that they will not be getting their money's worth for her time. She is not afraid to say, "I want you to know you do not have my full attention at this moment."

Autonomy in your work does not come without heavy dues, however. "You have to have a certain amount of power to choose your caseloads and be able to settle your cases. You have to prove to everybody that you're not afraid of a fight. At the beginning, I had to work hard just to stay afloat," she said. "I spun my wheels a lot. Then I figured out how to generate a living from the practice."

Her firm now employs four lawyers and four support staff, and selects its cases carefully. If a case will require extensive travel and intense evening and weekend work, the partners usually refer the case to another firm.

"Our culture at Samuel and Ballard is that you shouldn't have to work like a dog just because you're a lawyer."

PATIENTS VERSUS FAMILY

Depending on their professions, some entrepreneurs have no choice but to "work like a dog." Dr. Leslye Heilig spent four exhausting but fulfilling years as a solo pediatrician in the small, rural New York state town where she grew up. Her story closely resembles the portrait of the classic entrepreneur, who tastes the rewards and the exhaustion of round-the-clock immersion in a private venture. However, her catalyst for breaking out on her own had little to do with professional ambition and ego.

Leslye Heilig decided to uproot her family and move back to her hometown when her mother was diagnosed with metastatic cancer. "My sister, too, left her job, as a social worker, to run my parents' business. We each had three years to be close to our mother."

She opened her rural practice and, for the next four years, was the town's busiest pediatrician. Being a country doctor was professionally isolating, but Leslye adored her work.

"Becoming a solo practitioner was the best thing I ever did. I learned and matured a lot. I knew all my patients. I did exactly what I wanted in terms of how I set up my office. I really like being part of people's lives." She still receives long-distance calls from former patients.

Leslye's husband, a former investment adviser, had carried the major burden of child care since the couple's twin daughters were born during Leslye's residency. He continued to be the primary parent, and he was his wife's office manager, after their move to her hometown.

Even with such strong family support, Leslye and her husband decided to close the practice after four years. "I was on call every night. We had not taken a vacation in many years. Birthday parties always got interrupted."

She searched for a partner to share the practice, but could not find anyone suitable. Perhaps if she had found a colleague, she would not have felt forced to choose between her patients and her family. "I just could not be that effective as a wife and mother and also be a doctor to my patients 100 percent of the time."

Leslye has joined a small group practice in rural western Massachusetts, but she says she has no regrets about her four years on her own. Like many talented women who are making multiple career changes, Leslye did not want to be self-employed forever, but cherishes the chance she had to be her own boss.

THE FAMILY BUSINESS

Women may face a particularly complex challenge when they try literally to go home again—to run the family business.

Barbara Pearce has dual credentials from Harvard, in business and law, but she still felt forced to prove to herself, her father, and his company that she could manage the family real estate business as capably as a man.

She began her professional career as a corporate lawyer, but never intended to practice law forever. "The kind of law I was in was incompatible with family life of any kind. I did mergers and acquisitions, and traveled at the drop of a hat. Few of the women in the firm were married."

Barbara and her husband had a Boston/New York commuter marriage, which put additional strain on her already demanding calendar. She remembers the day her plane was grounded on a runway in New York and she waited in her own personal fog from the wear and tear of her frenzied schedule. She had to ask the passenger sitting next to her which direction the plane was headed.

As Barbara began to question the sanity of her own lifestyle, her father was planning his retirement from his real estate development firm in Connecticut. Barbara and her husband wanted to start a family, which made becoming her own boss more appealing. Yet her wish to combine work and family became a controversial point for her father, who was initially skeptical about the depth of her professional commitment. He supported her ambition, but wondered whether a person can vary from a traditional schedule and still be taken seriously.

The Managerial Woman, one of the first studies of career women, reflected similar portraits of ambitious women, torn by the mixed signals they receive from their fathers. Today's professional woman has not found easy resolution of the conflict she faces over her double roles: ambition versus nurturing.

Her choices are even more difficult when those closest to her will not support her goals, or cannot figure out how to reconcile them.

Before he turned over his business to her, Barbara's father spoke with everyone in the company about his daughter. Their universal response was, "No woman can do the top job in commercial real estate."

Now she can laugh as she tells a classic anecdote about her father's skepticism during her early years of running the company. "People told him that he was too tough on me—that 40 hours was as much as he should expect from someone with kids. Then, trying to show how liberated he was, he said, 'It was different for me. I didn't have any kids.' Everyone looked at him and started to laugh."

Eight years after Barbara took the reins, her father resurveyed the group. This time they said, "She's tough enough—actually too tough, tougher than you were." Barbara readily admits, "I'm more sensitive to people trying to bully me."

The firm, based in New Haven, employs 150 people in seven sites. It has taken Barbara 10 years of the traditional long hours to feel comfortable with her current fluid, nontraditional schedule, even though she knows she has paid her dues. She picks her children up at school at 3:00 P.M. most days but puts in a 40- to 50-hour week by working early in the morning and most nights.

Her first child was born on a Friday, and she returned to work on Monday. She decided not to take a maternity leave because she wanted to prove her professional commitment to her father and her company. "I had only been in the business a couple of years, and I wanted people to think I was serious about working. I was concerned that people would think that I wasn't."

Even her father believed she would change her mind about running the business after she became a mother. "He's still not convinced that women with children can be major players. He is prone to say, 'Most women can't run a business, but my daughter can.' "

Neither Barbara's family life nor her work style is typical. "My family seldom sits down to dinner together. Once, when my son saw a picture of a group sitting around a dinner table, he said, 'Look, Mom! A meeting!' He thinks I go to meetings and talk on the phone. He thinks my husband goes to work."

Barbara is one of the few working MBAs who is not in her office at 4:00 P.M. Being her own boss means her work schedule is fluid. She does her paperwork at night so that she can drop off and pick up her children from school during the day. We interviewed her in the late afternoon in her home, with the din of Looney Tunes cartoons in the background. However, as soon as she began to speak in her assertive, direct style, we dismissed any tendency to describe her as someone who has slowed down.

"Having children is a normal thing for businesswomen to do," she said, with emphasis. "Having children made me a much better manager. It made me more efficient and more tolerant of other people. I know I'm very threatening. I think it made me more human."

Barbara's self-employment also determined how she and her lawyer husband would divide family responsibilities. "My husband and I figured that only one of us could afford to be in a cyclical business, which is what real estate is. Our operating premise is that I would have flexibility. He reminds me of that when I say he isn't pulling his share of the load."

Family businesses are known for raising comparisons between one generation and the next. Barbara Pearce, however, holds no misgivings about the path she has chosen.

"I think that if I can raise happy, well-adjusted, healthy kids while running this business, that will be enough different from what my father did. I won't have to say that he was a bigger success than I was."

HUSBAND AND WIFE, INC.

A few of the women we surveyed are in business with their husbands. Many people might cringe at the notion of such constant connection, but the professional and personal marriage works for some successful entrepreneurs.

From the third floor of their sprawling Victorian home, Jane Duncan,* MBA, and her husband run a consulting business to Fortune 100 companies. Her background in investment banking and his contacts as a business school professor give them ideal credentials for a business partnership.

"There's no question," Jane Duncan says. "I could never go back and work for someone else. If I were doing exactly the same activity for a consulting firm, I would make a third as much money. I don't have overhead to pay, and I'm not being paid by someone else who has overhead to pay. We do hire others to work for us—but only on a project-by-project basis."

Among the women we interviewed, Jane Duncan was an exception in earning more than she would in a traditional setting. But even for her, the main incentive for self-employment is not financial.

"This allows me the flexibility to work the hours I want—and I couldn't do that anywhere else," Jane says. Others might find her schedule chaotic, but she does her best work in small chunks of time, with lots of breaks for her children throughout the day. She drives her older child to school at 9:00 A.M. and picks her up at 1:00 P.M., then works upstairs for a few hours while her live-in help watches the children. At 3:00, Jane spends about two hours doing errands with the children and driving them to activities. After their bedtime at 8:30, she sits down at her desk for another hour or two of work.

Jane's daughter has a desk, well-stocked with crayons, paper, and a toy typewriter, at which she can join her mother in the office on a slow workday. "The time I put in is broken up,

*An asterisk after a name designates a pseudonym.

but it's efficient time," Jane said. "There are also times when this whole thing goes upside down, and I work around the clock. And there are other times when I'm doing nothing."

Unlike most of the women we met, Jane has been able to schedule some leisure time for herself. "I love sports, and I can run out during the day for a game of paddle tennis and then go right back to work."

Even with this seemingly ideal balance in her life, she says, "When we really have a lot of work to do, there is frustration, chaos, and stress—and all of this is felt *in the house*. Sometimes I say I should just get an office around the corner, but I know I wouldn't ever do it."

The professional isolation, the risk, no one to pass your work on to—each drawback can make the small-scale entrepreneur wonder sometimes whether what she is doing makes sense. Yet she knows, from vivid past experience, that anything other than self-employment would not let her move as comfortably between her roles as mother and professional.

THE OFFICE IN THE HOME

Perhaps you have seen the commercial starring the mother dressed in jeans, who picks up one of her phone lines as she removes a printout from her fax machine. Then the image cuts to a noontime shot of her three-year-old bouncing into the kitchen for a glass of milk. The mother says, smiling, "I thought I'd miss those power lunches, but now I have lunch with more important people."

This commercial, selling expanded business telephone services, calls up just the right image for potential buyers. Its message is that technology can readily solve the obstacles to successful, satisfying employment based in the home.

The ad agency was right on one count. Technology is removing the traditional communication barriers to conducting professional business from home. But technology does not tell the whole story; neither does the commercial. While it dispels one set of assumptions about where work has to get done, it also perpetuates the myth that the mother "working" at home is really playing with her child.

Every entrepreneur we met, whether she worked in her home or in an office, had arranged the best and most dependable child care available. In many cases, they also had negotiated backup care. Each woman clearly understood and respected the invisible divider between home and work; each set clear limits for how she balanced her time between the two.

The telephone commercial did get one thing right, however. Not one woman we surveyed expressed any regrets for missing the power lunches when she "dropped out." The powerful combination of disillusionment with the male rules of the game and the desire to find a better way to make a living has fueled the determination of women who want to carve out their own standards for success.

There was a time, not too long ago, when Janet Shur thought she had made a mistake in becoming a lawyer. "I really hated it. I didn't like the travel—and I hated being a litigator, arguing with people, manipulating them, figuring out how to outsmart them."

Now Janet runs a thriving tax-law practice with her partner, a former 1970s commune mate. Almost in spite of herself, she has succeeded professionally, without the trappings of a traditional law practice or a big ego.

Janet, dressed in sweater and slacks, greeted us in her office in her partner's rambling house in Cambridge, Massachusetts. A dog ran through the living room as Janet described her firm's first 10 years. The partnership is so successful that the women regularly turn away business, to protect the part-time, flexible schedule that each believes is crucial for her role as a mother.

After passing the bar, Janet went to work as a litigator for a national children's rights organization. Five years in a "burnout" profession made her realize that she did not want to end up like the lawyers with whom she worked. "They worked constantly. Their careers were the most important things in their lives. They were really doing a lot of good for children, but the personal cost—for me anyway—seemed very high."

Janet's transition to another career began with a six-month stint as a biology field researcher in the Galápagos Islands, followed by a part-time job as a hearing officer for the Massachusetts Department of Education.

"Then it became clear that I was going to have to go back to work and make money again. I actually considered a total career change. When I thought about whether there was anything in law I liked, I realized I had always enjoyed doing other people's taxes."

Luck and timing combined for her. Janet's long-time friend (and now law partner) Elizabeth Edmunds was also looking for a way to spend more time with her children. Now these two attorneys work 50-hour weeks only during tax season. The rest of the year they carry half to two-thirds of a normal client load (although both women are always accessible to clients by phone).

Chemistry and a shared sense of values about work and family are the keys to the Shur-Edmunds partnership. Their time as housemates in a 1970s Cambridge commune had given them the chance to work out most of the issues that people don't realize are "partnership issues," Janet said. "That's why it was such a good match."

Each woman recognizes how difficult it is to form a partnership that works so well. They quickly dismiss any occasional thoughts about bringing in another partner to handle the business they turn away.

Now that their practice is well established, Janet can chuckle at the initial reactions of some of her clients. "Almost all our work is referrals. Sometimes the first interview will be a little uncomfortable as they're sizing us up. One thing Harvard did for me—and it shouldn't necessarily be this way, but it's the public perception—is that, when clients ask me where I went to law school and I say, 'Harvard,' they stop worrying. They don't care if I'm wearing jeans and they've come to a house instead of a big, fancy office. They say, 'Oh, Harvard. Then you must know what you're doing.' That's a real luxury. I don't have to prove myself to a new client.''

Janet readily acknowledges that working a reduced work-week for most of the year means a serious financial sacrifice. She is the primary parent at home, both because she is the secondary wage earner and because this choice reflects the importance of balance in her life. Regardless of the sacrifices, control over her working environment and her unusual schedule makes self-employment the only choice for her.

Janet fits in an hour's work before her three-year-old daughter, Anna, wakes at 7:00 A.M. "Then I'll try to be a mother for an hour or so." She is somewhat apologetic for having so much flexibility. "I just take it for granted. The only time I realize what a luxury it is, is when I talk to other women. Yesterday morning my partner's daughter was singing in a school assembly, and Betsy [her partner] and I both went to it."

Self-employment does not entirely do away with working-mother guilt, though it certainly helps it to subside a bit. Janet Shur says that she has been very lucky in her work situation, but she still faces the usual guilt and occasional self-doubt about her role as working mother.

"Looking at me from the outside, you would say, 'This is the ideal job, balancing work and family.' Well, you know, I still feel guilty half the time because I'm not with Anna as much as I should be."

LOGGING THE HOURS

Reducing the workweek may be out of the question, even for entrepreneurs who can build flexibility into their schedules and maintain some control over when and where they put in their hours.

MBA Eleanor Latimer works as many hours as possible—typically from 8:30 A.M. to 6:00 P.M. in Latimer Ventures, the home-based consulting practice she founded for venture capital health care companies.

Eleanor describes herself as a "displaced New Englander," who has moved back and forth between the East Coast and Texas several times in the last 10 years to accommodate her husband's transfers and promotions. When she left her corporate job in New York and relocated to Fort Worth, Texas, she felt severe culture shock as she hunted for a job. "I'm a very typical New Englander and very direct. It's a different culture here. It's a macho world. I was a threat to men."

After trying four companies in four years, and because of the unfortunate combination of bad luck and poor timing, Eleanor began to feel that her career was going far off track. "I said, 'The heck with it. I'm not going to work for anyone else—and I'm not going to let this place beat me.' "

She is ready for the possibility that her family may move again. "My business is totally portable. I can take it anywhere. All I need to have is a telephone. In fact, most of my clients are on the East Coast."

Being her own boss gives Eleanor "tremendous flexibility" and the freedom to get involved in family life. She can be active in her children's school fund-raising (she recently raised $100,000), can greet her children when they come home from school, and can take time in the middle of the day to call her mother, whose health she monitors from a distance.

When the children return from school, Eleanor spends some time with them as her version of a coffee break, but she is also disciplined about closing the door of her "office"—the guest bedroom—and turning the children over to the care of their nanny.

Full-time, live-in child care is critical to her professional success, because Eleanor does not get paid for any time that she does not work. "I can usually work from home, but I do end up traveling a couple of times a month, sometimes on short notice. I will literally have to drop everything to go on a business trip. I could not consider it without full-time, live-in help."

Eleanor also feels strongly that at least one parent needs flexibility for the time it takes to be involved in children's activities. "I am the primary parent. My husband is in the oil business and not at home very much. Somebody's got to be the parent. I'm the Cub Scout den mother. I teach Sunday school. My life is their life."

Some might view Eleanor's profession as simply trading one set of stresses for another, but she is persuasive in describing the circumstances that make self-employment her only realistic career choice.

"Nobody is looking over my shoulder—ever. My clients alone judge my work—and they come back." Although Eleanor tells us she "couldn't be busier," she is about to set in motion the concept for another business she wants to start.

PUTTING FAMILY FIRST

Sacrificing ambition for more control and independence in her work can mean giving up a woman's financial autonomy at home. Forsaking a paycheck equal to her husband's may seem like a step backward for women like Janet Shur, who know that they are as capable professionally as their husbands. The women we surveyed, however, seem so comfortable with their decision to put family first that they don't feel that they are in the subordinate role in the home that most of their mothers occupied. These women are spending time at home by choice. Most said they do not miss the traditional and fast-track professional lives they left behind. In short, they are doing exactly what they want.

"Those 'mommy emotions' and hormones really surprised me," said MBA Barbara Keck, who runs her own industrial marketing consulting firm from her home in California. "They *made* my decision to work at home." Reflecting on how she and her husband contemplated their work/family merger, Barbara comments: "We cried and talked and went through a year of 'negotiation.' My spouse agreed that I could work full-time as a mother if I wanted. But *I* made the choice to 'stay home and work.' Wise choice? Maybe. Hindsight has its benefits. But I'll never know how far I could have gone. . . ."

Barbara faced a tough choice after her maternity leave: be laid off as a part-timer or return to a traditional 60-hour week. She had worked for four years as a marketing manager at Continental Can in California, and planned to propose a part-time schedule for her return. While she was on leave, however, her company faced a 30 percent reduction in force. Because reduction was based on head count numbers, part-time work was not an option.

Barbara decided to do something nontraditional for a Harvard MBA: to leave the corporate world, *and* work part-time, *and* not make a lot of money. During her pregnancy, she announced her plans for a career change to the women's management association she headed—and met unexpected and angry resistance from other professional women.

"Well, Barbara," a fellow board member told her, "I'm not sure how it would look to the outside world if an executive woman, who had her first child and intends not to return to corporate life, still held a leadership role in this organization." (That woman later chose to stay at home when she became a mother.)

One month after the birth of her first child, Barbara opened her consulting business, where her "office" is "a short commute from the kitchen and laundry." Most of the time, Barbara Keck works from 8:30 A.M. to 3:00 P.M., spends afternoon time with her 11-year-old and 9-year-old children, then returns to work from 4:30 P.M. to 6:00 P.M. As a solo practitioner, she has learned to go with the flow, with a work load that can vary from a 20- to a 90-hour week. When the overload gets too heavy, she subcontracts work to other "MBA moms." Giving herself the credit she deserves for learning to adjust to the varying hours, she comments, "I have learned to cherish the valleys. (I challenge a man to be able to do that!) And I feel somewhat guilty about [the time I spend on] the peaks."

"I work what most Harvard MBAs would consider a part-time job. Everyone I know is putting in somewhere between 10- to 14-hour days. I don't know anyone who holds down an executive position in an 8-hour day."

She dismisses the notion that "quality time" makes up for 14-hour workdays. "There is a *quantity* of time involved as well as quality. I think that a full-time job just doesn't allow you to meet some basic emotional needs for your children."

Barbara does feel some regret at giving up her executive position. "There's some hurt pride in making less money. And now that I've stepped off the corporate rolls, my sense of being able to reenter, especially after age 40, is remote. Regrets? Yes, sometimes. Self-image is very much tied up with my work, and so it's a constant and daily struggle to try and do it all well." Yet she knows she has made the right decision about how she has chosen to be a mother.

Unfortunately, a depressed economy is changing Barbara's range of choices. Her husband, an investment banker, recently was laid off. "The glory days of investment banking are over," Barbara says with a sigh. "There's no way my husband is going to pull in the income he did before. So I need to give serious consideration to whether or not I can make a lot of money in my own business and make up that gap, or go to work for someone else and have that income insurance."

Even if the worst case happens and Barbara has to give up her current flexibility, she says she has no regrets about the entrepreneurial years. They have given her the kind of time she wanted to have with her children. Barbara's counsel to other mothers: "Do what you think is right at the time. Try to listen to your own counsel, not to peer pressure. Will you have regrets about whatever your choice? Absolutely. That's life. But when you are on your deathbed, and the rattle is in your throat, don't expect corporate America to be there. But maybe your family *will* be there."

THE RIGHT STUFF

For many entrepreneurs, neither poetic inspiration nor an idealized fantasy about being the boss moved them to build a business from scratch. Their springboard to self-employment was a deep frustration with the traditional careers and all-consuming work environment for which they had been so well groomed at Harvard.

Today these women are their own bosses. They may not be able to work fewer hours than they did in their traditional professional roles, but they are always in charge of calling the shots.

The myth of the fast-paced high roller, devoured by her work, does not hold for the entrepreneurial woman who is also managing a family. Self-employment is not as glamorous as it might appear from the outside, but it can be both satisfying and sane. The entrepreneurs we surveyed offered behind-the-scenes conclusions about what it really means to strike out on your own:

- **Not all entrepreneurs make huge amounts of money.** The degree of control you gain over your career, however, is immeasurable—in fact, priceless.

- **Financial rewards may be lower—or merely delayed.** Savings from your single and childless years can be critical to founding your own venture. Financial support from your spouse can make it easier to take the risk and may actually be essential during the start-up phase of your business.

- **Some aspects of self-employment are just plain hard.** If you work alone, you may suffer some professional isolation—offset, however, by the freedom to set your own terms for your organization.

- **Even entrepreneurs go through a "proving stage."** Establish a solid professional reputation in a more traditional work setting before going it alone. The early years can be both a training ground and a strategy for lessening the proving stage of your own enterprise. It may take awhile for both you and your clients to feel truly confident about your nontraditional approach. However, if you have the right technology—regular telephone contact and a good fax machine—clients need never know that you are working in your jeans from your home.

- **Dependable child care is essential.** In fact, stable child care is even *more* critical for working mothers who do not receive paid vacations and who, as one-person ventures, may have no backup to serve their clients.

- **Becoming an entrepreneur does not necessarily mean you will be able to go it alone completely.** Without professional backup, you can still have some flexibility, but it may be impossible to reduce your hours. Being your own boss can be invigorating, though. Because your time is your own, you can be as efficient as you want—with no one to slow you down.

- **All maternal guilt does not disappear with self-employment.** However, mothers who have control over their schedules can attend a school play or stay at home with a sick child without having to make apologies to a boss or a co-worker.

There is something heady about striking out on your own and doing what you truly love, even if autonomy means giving up some of your early professional ambitions. Most of the self-employed women we surveyed readily acknowledged that their paychecks are lower than in the past but the overall quality of their lives is quite high and very full. Energized by the control that comes with being your own boss, they end their workdays less fatigued for the home front than when they were in a traditional work setting.

Entrepreneurs may not be able to "have it all," but they are proving that they can come very close to revoking the Diana Penalty. These women feel that they will always need to prove themselves to someone. As entrepreneurs, they can prove themselves to *themselves*, to a carefully chosen partner, and to their own clients. As their own bosses, they can create *their own* proving ground—and hold the apologies.

CHAPTER SIX

◆ ◆ ◆

Putting Ambition on Hold: Full-Time Moms

"I stopped working full-time when I asked myself why, when I had two wonderful children [whom] I loved, was I leaving the house at 8 and getting home at 6 every day? My children were being raised by a wonderful, caring person . . . my housekeeper, not by me."
> —AUDREY KADIS, MIT 1970,
> HARVARD BUSINESS SCHOOL 1977

"Deciding to quit my job after my third child was born was extremely difficult for me. I was torn between conflicting feelings of what I 'should' do—my obligations to my clients, to my children, and my sense of who I am."
> —DVEERA SEGAL, SUNY 1975, MA 1977,
> HARVARD LAW SCHOOL 1979

"Dropping out." "Copping out." Negative images about giving up and not being able to compete. For many women who decide to leave the work force to be full-time mothers, however, these images are dead wrong. These women *can* compete and advance, but they have decided that the price of having it all at the same time is too steep. They cringe when someone suggests that they are turning back the clock of progress for working women. They know they can still have long working lives, with plenty of years to reappear as professionals. For now, their immediate and pressing personal goal is to be full-time parents.

Other women, with fewer choices, are still being forced out of professions that will not allow them to work anything less than 12-hour days. Even if they leave the work force voluntarily, many apologize, from guilt or even embarrassment, for not working. These women are burdened by their own perception that, in going home full-time, they somehow have let down other women of their generation.

Now that professional women are leaving the work force in noticeable numbers, the mass media have identified a new "women versus women" syndrome, which pits working mothers against stay-at-home moms. "Housewife." "Career woman." Opposite ends of the female spectrum. The one suggests the persistent cartoon character in scruffy slippers, curled up on the living room couch, watching her soap operas; the other, a sharp-nailed dragon lady, married to her career, briefcase clutched to her chest.

Neither portrait is flattering; neither is accurate—and no such extreme images exist to pressure men to defend how they choose to lead *their* lives.

Media attention on parenting issues magnifies the guilt that each group of mothers may feel for their choices. Women at home may feel defensive about having taken a place in a competitive graduate school from someone who would have remained on the fast track. Mothers who continue working may question their decision not to be a "traditional" mom. Their ambivalence may grow as they hear stories about a new breed of "dropouts," women who are rediscovering the joys of motherhood and finding personal fulfillment as school volunteers and community activists.

Not every mother has the option of deciding to stay at home. The women we surveyed reminded us that, because of their husbands' incomes or their own investments and savings, they have more choices than do most women with children.

They were careful to point out that their decision to drop out involved long discussions with their husbands about the economic impact of living on only one salary. Some have since discovered that sacrificing their financial independence hit them much harder than they had anticipated—although they unanimously said that full-time motherhood has been the right choice for them.

• • •

One MBA mother who left the work force when her second child was born concludes: "It is simply not possible to pursue most highly demanding business or professional careers and be involved in the lives of your children, especially the elementary-aged children who need guidance, care, and discipline that baby-sitters cannot provide."

• • •

Another MBA mom spoke of how the norms and rules of business are stacked against parents who want to be involved with their children. "When I went to Harvard Business School, I was told you could have it all— career, marriage, family. No one told me *how* to do it." When she first stopped working, she says, "I felt like a failure because I wasn't using my education." Three years later she has come to terms with her decision, and adds, "This past spring my six-year-old was in the hospital with pneumonia. It made me realize that until my children are older, full-time work is out of the question for me."

• • •

Not surprisingly, the MBA moms in our survey, who face a more unyielding work culture than do lawyers or physicians, are the most likely to drop out. A surprising 25 percent of the Harvard MBAs have left the work force compared with 11 percent of the lawyers and 4 percent of the doctors. Some say that they plan to return to work as soon as their children are in elementary school; others say they plan to be at home indefinitely. None can predict how this choice will finally affect their work histories. Most wonder whether the road map to their careers will show a turn into a dead-end street because of their decision to be at home.

Why do women leave the work force? Would they have stayed if their companies had been more supportive of their needs as parents? How do they adjust to life at home after having been in a career for so long? How do their families adjust? When, and under what conditions, will they return to work? How do they prepare for reentry into their professions?

Unlike the entrepreneurs and the fast-trackers, the full-time mothers in our survey do not form a common portrait. Their lives are calmer, less stressful, and less guilt ridden, but they say that not every aspect of being at home is ideal. Each woman has gained something important to her, but many said that they have also felt a loss in another aspect of their lives. For example, a lawyer, who enjoyed more than 10 years away from the workplace, faces a cruel awakening as she goes through a divorce and discovers how unemployable she has become.

For many women and their families, part-time professional work would have been the best possible answer. A second income would have eased the strain placed on their husbands as sole breadwinners. Remaining in the work force would have helped the women maintain their own career-based self-esteem and financial independence, as well as their professional skills. However, the rigid work ethic in business, law, and medicine— with business being the most unyielding—has forced out some talented women whose first choice was *not* dropping out, but finding satisfying part-time work.

Dropping out is rarely a quick, clear-cut decision. Careful

soul-searching, experimenting with a reduced work schedule, and recognizing that one's career has become just a job are part of the long, often painful process. Do women want to return to the clearly defined roles of past generations, with mothers at home and fathers at work? No! Do we think that this apparent rise in professional dropouts is the wave of the future? Absolutely not! What, then, is the meaning of this exodus of top-flight professionals to a life-style that most would never have planned or predicted?

HITTING THE WALL

In her controversial 1990 commencement address at Wellesley College, Barbara Bush spoke of the opportunity "to cherish your human connections" and advised the new alumnae:

> *"For several years, you've had impressed upon you the importance to your career of dedication and hard work. This is true, but as important as your obligations as a doctor, lawyer, or a business leader will be, you are a human being first and those human connections—with spouses, with children, with friends—are the most important investments you will ever make. At the end of your life, you will never regret not having passed one more test, not winning one more verdict, or not closing one more deal. You will regret time not spent with a husband, a friend, a child, or a parent."*[1]

Barbara Bush struck a chord with mothers who could find some comfort in the simple concept of putting family first. Many of the dropouts we surveyed pointed to the fragility of their human connections and their pressing need to take full control of their lives by redirecting their priorities for home and work. The downside of the Barbara Bush message rests in its premise that women must make an either-or choice between the love they feel for their children and the desire for a rewarding, and usually economically necessary, career. Even if women are able to leave the work force for a while, most mothers cannot afford to do so for the long term.

For MBA Audrey Kadis, doing it all meant feeling tired all the time and increasingly frustrated at missing too much of her children's growing up. "With the women's movement, there was this promise held out that you could do everything. And for a long time I grappled with that and felt ripped off and angry. From the outside, and only from the outside, I did have it all."

Audrey describes herself as a full-time mom, but she is not at home all the time. She volunteers 15 hours a week at the AIDS Action Committee in Boston and continues to work as a personal financial planner for about 6 hours a week.

The day Audrey decided to tell her children that she was planning to stay at home full-time, her 10-year-old daughter looked her straight in the eye and said, "But, Mom, you can't do that! You don't have any experience."

The transition has not always been idyllic. "It has taken a full year of on-the-job training for my performance to equal that of my last housekeeper," Audrey says. "She knew my children's friends better than I did."

As Audrey walked past the bicycles parked in her dining room, she talked of having time now for leisurely bike rides with her two children. Dressed comfortably in jeans and sneakers, she led us to the kitchen of her large, yellow Victorian house in a Boston suburb and described the event that crystallized the choice she needed to make.

Two years ago a close friend and former Harvard Business School classmate called Audrey from Children's Hospital to say that her six-month-old son was about to undergo surgery for a brain tumor. "Fortunately, the surgery was successful, but I realized I was the only person who was there for her, except for her parents and mother-in-law," Audrey said.

"My friend had never had the time to cultivate any other friendships. When this terrible thing happened to her baby, she had no support system. And I couldn't help but think of my own wonderful, healthy children, who were being raised by someone else."

For Audrey, a financial planner and former software development manager, this experience sharply focused an idea that had been at the back of her mind for a long time. "I decided right then and there to stop working."

When she left her job, she realized how exhausted she had been, juggling career and family. "It was an enormous relief to have all this pressure taken off me." However, her first few months at home brought isolation and unanticipated restlessness. "I went out to lunch and did stuff I assume people at home full-time do. It was really boring." As is the case for many mothers at home, living in a neighborhood that emptied out completely for the 9- to-5 shift contributed to Audrey's initial sense of isolation.

Then, on the day before New Year's Eve, Audrey's brother called. "He told me he was HIV positive." Within a month, Audrey began to volunteer at the AIDS Action Committee two days a week while her children were in school. Her commitment to the organization runs deep. "Pretty soon I was there every spare minute I had. It turns out that what they really needed was help with corporate fund-raising." With quiet pride, she added, "I got 20 new companies to help, and raised about $50,000 in six months."

Like many women who leave careers for full-time motherhood, Audrey Kadis has seen a change in the rhythm of her family's life. They "just seem to operate on a different time and speed," she said. She remembers how difficult it was to focus fully on her children when she worked full-time and also had to think about errands, cooking, laundry, and paying bills in the evening.

Audrey vividly recalls her guilt during her first week at

home, when her daughter revealed how much she missed their housekeeper. "I feel like I lost my mother and father," the child said. "She was the one I talked to when I had problems."

For the most part, Audrey is at peace with her decision to alter radically her original life plans. Sometimes, however, she says, "I feel funny about not working. When I filled out a school form, they asked my occupation. I thought, How do you put down 'very part-time' or 'volunteer'? I think volunteering is really looked down upon. People don't take it very seriously. I put down 'consultant.' I lied." Her husband, however, proudly calls her a trendsetter for having the courage to follow her personal instincts.

Audrey hopes to be at home for years. "I look at my son, who is a preadolescent, and at how complicated it is, what he is going through socially. And I know it will get much worse for him in the next few years. I know that in our community, the kids are into drugs, sex, alcohol—all kinds of things that have real risks associated with them. I don't want my kids coming home to an empty house every afternoon. I want to be here for him if he has a problem at school. I can't change what happens at school, but [I hope] I can help him keep his self-esteem."

Audrey Kadis left the corporate world to spend more time with her children. When she returns to the work force, she knows she will not be seeking the corner office. She is passionate in her belief that her work for AIDS Action is for "a greater good" than anything she has ever done for a paycheck. She has decided that whatever she does for the rest of her life, paid or unpaid, it will be to give something back to society.

The money she raises at the AIDS Action Committee will be used to reach out to teenagers at risk or to help someone die with dignity. "At the Business School, no one ever discussed these kinds of things. They only talked about investment banking," Audrey says.

Women just starting out should be more realistic about career aspirations than she was, she advises. "Being a mother takes time—quality and 'nonquality' time. A serious professional career takes time—evenings, weekends, travel. And there are only 24 hours in a day. No matter how competent you are, you can't have a 30-hour day."

FROM MADISON AVENUE TO LIFE ON A FARM

MBA Priscilla Vincent has made career sacrifices that she never, in her wildest dreams, considered as she completed the grueling two-year program at the Harvard Business School. She could not have predicted that she would so willingly give up her Madison Avenue goals for a quiet family life on a small farm.

Feisty, energetic, and articulate, Priscilla seems a natural for a fast-track career in advertising. She loved her job. "My company was a wonderful place to work. They treated their people like the finest people in the world, and they performed like the finest." But advertising is a high-pressure, frenzied business. "It took your body and soul."

To balance work and family demands, Priscilla planned each detail of her life. She and her husband would leave their house by 7:15 A.M. each morning, drop their children at the day-care center, then drive to the other side of town to the train station. Knowing she would not take time for lunch, Priscilla would grab breakfast at a coffee shop in the city and arrive at her desk by 8:15 A.M.

Because the evening train home did not get in until after the day-care center closed, Priscilla paid a baby-sitter to pick up her children, take them home, and feed them dinner. At home again 12 hours after they had left, Priscilla and her husband would play with the children, put them to bed and, at 9:00 P.M., look at each other and say, "What are we going to do about dinner?"

In her straightforward, no-nonsense style, Priscilla described the physical and mental toll of her hectic schedule. "I found I was staring at the wall a lot at work, and I knew I was not performing mentally. Outwardly, I was going through the motions and doing a great job, but inwardly I was losing it. I tried to tell my boss that I was not doing my best work, but he resisted the idea of my quitting.''

For a year and a half after her second child was born, Priscilla denied her feelings that either something in her life had to give or she would be sentencing herself to total burnout. Advertising was in her blood. Even after her return from a second maternity leave, she found her work with clients ''intoxicating.'' She kept hoping that someone else would tell her she had to leave her job. She even went to her doctor for a general checkup, hoping he would, in effect, give her permission to quit by telling her that she had to slow down.

Priscilla found she had to put herself on automatic pilot just to get through each day. ''I got so I couldn't focus my eyes at the end of the day. I was exhausted all the time. I really knew I had to get out.'' Yet she also was ''terrified'' that she would not know what to do as a full-time mother.

Chicken pox nearly put her over the edge. When her two young children came down with the disease, Priscilla had only two options: take several weeks off from work or ask her mother to fly cross-country to take care of the children. She realized how fragile her family support system had become and how vulnerable she was to any breakdowns in the complicated logistics of her daily life.

Like many women who decide to leave the workplace, Priscilla had enough self-understanding to realize that she had ''put on the shelf'' one aspect of her identity to allow herself to succeed in another. Her transition from fast-tracker and superwoman to full-time mom was not automatic. She had deliberately waited to have children until she had achieved career success. Now she worried whether she would be able to find her ''other self,'' to learn how to relate to her children on a different level. She at first found her confidence as a mother undermined by serious questions about her role expectations, values, and life goals.

Although she enjoyed much of the headiness that comes with a fast-track profession, Priscilla says of her role as a full-time mom, "I feel less impoverished than when I was paid to work." As she reflected on her advertising days, she was interrupted by the sound of hay being mowed on the small farm where she lives with her husband and three children in rural Massachusetts. She never imagined that she would be growing and selling hay part-time rather than making her way on Madison Avenue.

Priscilla Vincent says she feels "like a dinosaur saying this, but my mother was right. A family is a full-time job." She quickly adds, "At the same time, I would vehemently support a woman's right to work and the necessity for equal opportunity. I used my graduate training for seven years, and I think I made a real contribution to my company and my clients." Her own children are benefiting from her work experience, she says, because it affects the way she functions in daily life. "They see the strength and skills I acquired. They absorb my values."

FOR THE SAKE OF HER CHILD

Attorney Katherine Griffith* fit the portrait of a full-time working woman. When her son was born, she seemed to have all the right pieces in place. Her own mother had worked full-time while rearing three children, and Katherine remembers her own childhood as happy. "Things seemed to work out so well for my mother. I was smug about my own life and said, 'My mother was a working parent, and I want to go back to work.'"

A graduate of Barnard College and Harvard Law School, Katherine had had 13 years of work experience when she took

*An asterisk after a name designates a pseudonym.

a 6-month maternity leave. When she told her husband that she wanted to go back to work, he said, "Of course, you need to. I'm a reference librarian. I can't support the family." For the next nine months, her husband stayed home while she returned to a four-day workweek.

At first Katherine tried to negotiate a week of fewer than the 35 to 40 hours she crammed into her four days, but was told that her boss would automatically reject the idea. "I felt the 'part-time' designation was meaningless because my boss gave me an unrealistic work load," she said. "I couldn't possibly have done what she wanted during a four-day week."

Her husband returned to work to a job that was slower paced and more part-time than her own, but the couple still had to put their son into day care for a large portion of the week. The thought that someone other than a parent was raising their child caused Katherine's guilt to escalate. "Besides the anguish of missing time with my son . . . when he was under two years old, steadily losing weight (to his pediatrician's alarm), and sick every three weeks—which caused me to miss a week of work each time. I was hopelessly behind at work and felt we were all suffering."

Like Priscilla Vincent, Katherine at first could not give herself the go-ahead to quit her job. Then her mother came to visit, took one look at her grandson, and said, "I can see this child doesn't belong in day care." This was the same grandmother who had always proclaimed that day care was a good experience for children.

The assessment gave Katherine "permission" to leave the work force. Her mother also offered financial help to allow the family to live without Katherine's salary and to deal with her son's medical diagnosis of "failure to thrive."

Katherine is somewhat embarrassed at finding herself, at 41, relying on her parents, but she knows she did the right thing. "My parents spent a fortune to send me to seven years of Ivy League schools, and now they have to support me. But my child still has problems, and they need to be resolved." Her husband also feels "very inadequate" about not making more money, but each recognizes that a high-pressure profession would never have permitted his paternity leave or his part-time schedule.

Katherine Griffith has a new baby now; her older son needs two more years of intensive therapy, and Katherine is thinking of making a career change to teaching when her boys enter elementary school. Like Audrey Kadis's experience, Katherine's version of "hitting the wall" has become the catalyst for a new career and new choices about how she wants to lead her life.

ESCAPE FROM THE BLUE SUITS

MBA Marty Wallace had always assumed that she would be able to combine career and family successfully, but the truth was "I felt I was missing too much of my son's growing up." Now a mother of two, Marty quit her job as a software development manager when she began to believe her role as a parent was suffering. "My role as a mother was something that, when it was gone—that is, my children grown—it was gone forever. A career is renewable. Kids are kids for just a couple of years, and that's it."

From her graceful Tudor home in a Boston suburb, Marty says, "It took two years to be really comfortable with staying home. A lot of it has to do with my view of who I am. I never pictured myself at home with kids. When I would see other mothers at home with their children, I would say, 'What's wrong with them? Don't they have anything better to do with their lives?' Now I've joined that crowd."

Marty's transition, from working woman who would travel "at the drop of a hat" to full-time mom, was bumpy at times. To eliminate travel, she moved from a line position in computer installations to a staff position in marketing. First she tried working three days a week, then moved up to four. Throughout her changes, she felt her company was behind her; in fact, the company let her define both her job and her hours after her return from maternity leave.

Marty was lucky in at least having the option of part-time work, but this was not the best answer for her own work/family dilemma. When she stopped being a principal decision maker in her department, Marty lost what she considered critical professional rewards. "Career maintenance," when balanced with time away from her children, seemed too high a price.

Part-time work is not that great, Marty says. "You're kind of half there and not there. They don't really integrate you. If your aspiration is to become a key member of the company, you're not going to do it on a part-time basis. Somewhere I dropped off the radar screen because I was working part-time."

As she glanced out the window toward the children's climbing structure in her side yard, Marty acknowledged that her quest to have it all made her "very grumpy" all the time. She really started to worry about what was happening to her personality when she heard her husband warn a friend coming to dinner, "Don't be offended if Marty's in a really bad mood. It only means she had *another* bad day at work."

Feeling tired and stressed from a job that had lost its rewards confirmed her decision to drop out. At times she misses being with other adults and the personal ego boost that came from being in the business world. The problem with being a mother, Marty jokes, is that "there's no career ladder, no positive feedback—except for a hug once in awhile."

For Harvard Business School-trained women like Marty Wallace, image is no small consideration. Many cannot easily give up the tangible rewards of clients and paychecks. However, we were particularly struck by the exceptionally high level of respect these women now accord themselves for their new—and challenging—role as full-time mom. They have cast themselves in the role of mother by choice, not by default to their husbands' role. This undoubtedly has helped them feel comfortable with their decision to leave the careers for which they had fought so hard.

GOODBYE, "GUNG HO CAREER"

Joanne Barrows* never expected to drop out. Before she had children, she worked "lawyer's hours": 8:00 A.M. to 7:00 P.M. plus most weekends. When her first child was born, she negotiated a reduced schedule of 8.00 A.M. to 4:00 P.M. "I was able to leave when I said I was going to leave, but there was a lot of pressure on me, mostly self-induced, that I wasn't doing enough or as much as other people were doing."

The turning point in Joanne's thinking came when her child-care arrangements for her toddler son fell apart. "I put an ad in the paper for somebody new, and I really couldn't shake the feeling that I was advertising for someone to give my child away to. Also, I was pregnant with our second. It seemed like a good time to quit."

Joanne has been a full-time mom since 1986 and says, from her Maryland home, that she never in a million years, as a "former gung ho career type," expected to leave her profession for so long. The transition can be very hard on the ego because of the loss of the clear "adult identity" provided by a career.

"Lawyers spend half their day complimenting one another—so there's a lot of ego massage, a lot of adult feedback. When you're not working, all of a sudden that's gone." When her younger child enters kindergarten, Joanne plans to find part-time work, mainly for financial reasons. She knows finding such a job will not be easy.

While the rewards of the workplace are clear and steady, it is easy for career "dropouts" to fall into the trap of looking to their husbands for ego gratification. The danger in this, Joanne Barrows says, is letting your husband become the adult who comes home every day and judges how you've done.

Be prepared to be bored at times, she cautions other mothers thinking about staying at home. Realize that your ego will suffer if you felt successful in your work. However, as she describes the unconditional love that she receives from her children, Joanne says of her own decision to drop out, "It has definitely been worth it."

FIRST CHOICE: PART-TIME WORK

After 10 years as a management consultant for Digital Equipment Corporation, Sara Johnson, MBA, found that her career choices as a new mother were all or nothing. The company's unspoken policy was that managers in her field could not work part-time. Sara decided to quit her job rather than accept a demotion after her maternity leave.

Her toddler son chattered happily throughout our interview, as his youthful-looking mom reflected on the choices she had made. "Having my first child at 40—after I became less ambitious in my career, having already achieved moderate success—makes me want to stay home rather than feel guilty or stressed."

Sara had consciously postponed childbearing earlier in her business career. Before her son was born, she did not know what she would decide to do about working. Her husband, a generation older, was more comfortable with the idea of her staying at home. Once she began her maternity leave, "I had a change of heart and decided not to go back to work. It just felt right." (Sleep deprivation alone seemed reason enough to quit.) "I don't know how people do it," she exclaimed.

Sara misses the social interaction of work and the independence of earning her own paycheck, but she is adamant that working full-time would be detrimental to her child. When her son begins school, she hopes to find a part-time position. She is not yet fully comfortable with the financial implications of staying at home.

"Our family has a lot less money. (My husband and I earned about the same.) Somehow, when you are not earning your own money, you feel like you have a lot less discretion about how you spend it. It's not mine."

How has she been able to combine career and family? Sara Johnson says simply, "First, I did one. Now I'm doing the other. A personal life cannot be 'put on hold,' while a career can. Children and husbands can easily be forgotten in the rush for career success, but they cannot be reclaimed."

RECLAIMING AMBITION: SEQUENCING AND REENTRY

Unfortunately, stepping off a career track may seem to confirm the persistent myth that women simply cannot compete in the workplace. The reality is that any parent—male or female—may not be able to have it all at the same time. Men have never done it "all" at once, nor have they been expected to try.

The practice of leaving a career, for family concerns or for other forms of self-fulfillment, is termed *sequencing*. Sequencing allows parents to move in and out of careers, depending on their families' needs and developmental stages. The idea seems to make so much sense—so why aren't more women doing it?

Unfamiliarity is the principal barrier to sequencing because it involves uncharted territory in professions based on continuous, lifelong employment. Some women hesitate about leaving the work force, even for a limited time, because they fear permanent and insurmountable repercussions. Even as they are leaving their jobs, they worry about what will happen when they return.

Marty Wallace, at home for 5 years, worries that she is becoming "rusty," given how rapidly the computer industry evolves. "It would be hard to say, 'Hire me. I'm a wonderful person. I've been doing grocery shopping and laundry for 10 years.' " In contrast to Marty's justifiable concerns about reentry, Audry Kadis is optimistic that her challenging and now

161

successful role of volunteer fund-raiser may lead to paid part-time work when her children are a bit older.

Other women we interviewed are taking active steps to ease their professional reentry.

Gloria Gaston, MD, is one of the few in our survey to have established a sequencing track record. She had a plan for moving in and out of a career, followed it, and it worked. After "five good years" at home with her children, now 7 and 10, she returned to a part-time solo practice in rheumatology in 1988.

Health concerns about her own family were the ironic catalyst for Gloria's taking a leave from medicine. Each time she dropped off her young son, who has asthma, at day care, she would come down hard on herself, asking, "What am I doing— going out to practice medicine—when I really should be practicing medicine right here at home?"

She also found herself getting sick with every ear and respiratory infection that her children brought home. On most days, she says, "I had already put in a full day's work at home before I even examined my first patient in the office." Even a four-day workweek at her community health maintenance organization did not give her enough time as a mother.

Being a mother is infinitely more challenging than anything she has ever done in medicine, Gloria says. "I didn't realize how much I identified with my profession. I was a doctor. I'd always been a doctor. It was the only thing I knew about."

Like many highly trained women, Gloria entered full-time motherhood with high expectations and some trepidation. Although she is generally upbeat and confident, she felt far from happy as a new mother. "At home, I was in an area I felt very uncomfortable with. I didn't know much about children. I never knew if I was doing it right or wrong. I didn't have any type of reward system. And I'd lost some of the independence I'd always had."

Gloria's first two years at home were difficult, but by the

third year she had "reidentified" herself and become a regular volunteer in her children's school. She still continues to teach fine arts appreciation in the public schools and assists with dissections in the school laboratory.

Gloria Gaston acknowledges that it is easier to reenter some medical specialties than others. To stay current in her own field before reentering in 1988, she read medical journals, attended medical conferences, and occasionally gave lectures in rheumatology. She would like to see society pay a higher tribute to roles performed in the home. "I have tremendous respect for women who stay at home and maintain a family," she says. The price she paid for being a mother "was a small fee with a great return." As a bonus for the time she spent at home, Gloria and her sons continue to accumulate karate belts in the classes they started taking together a few years ago.

FORCED CHOICE: BACK TO FULL-TIME

Lauren Kahn has "hit the wall" full force. Her divorce means that she must find secure and well-paying work after more than 10 years away from her profession. In her case, the forced choice means returning to the work force, rather than leaving it.

A former trial attorney for the U.S. Department of Justice, Lauren has no regrets about her 11 years at home with her children and as a regular volunteer in their school and synagogue. However, her new role as a single parent has brought harsh and discouraging economic realities. "I'm not sorry I stayed home with the kids. What I'm sorry about is, now that my marriage has disintegrated, I'm having a terrible time getting a job."

Lauren was one of about 35 women in her class of over 500 at Harvard Law School. When her daughter was a newborn, she succumbed to "all that women-are-as-good-as-men pressure"

163

and returned to work right away, to a weekly schedule of four 8-hour days. "I felt that if I didn't go back to work—and had taken a man's place in law school—I was betraying my education."

She thought about staying at home when her daughter was first diagnosed with a club foot. Her daughter's medical problems, which eventually involved five surgeries, meant that Lauren had to schedule all doctor appointments on her one day off. "I didn't feel right about being at work and finding someone to stay with her." The other concession she made for her new baby—giving up legal cases that involved travel—also meant that her career itself had become much less exciting. After two months back at work, she "threw in the towel" and chose full-time motherhood.

Now she finds her current job interviews depressing. "If they find out I'm a single parent, that makes them leery. They assume that I'm going to have child-care problems. And the fact that I have been home for so long works against me. There are so many out-of-work lawyers. Firms are closing down. My experience is ancient."

This stressful period has heightened Lauren's disillusionment about a woman's ability to dedicate herself to a profession and still be there to raise her children. She advises other women, "Be realistic in thinking about the long-term implications of what you do—not only for your children, but for yourself."

Lauren understandably sounds discouraged when she says, "If you continue in a demanding job, it will be detrimental to your home life. If you quit or reduce hours, you'll have trouble finding a job when you decide to return to work full-time." Yet, despite her ambivalence about her own life choices, she stresses, "All you can do is make the right decision for today."

Now facing the financial bind of a single parent, Lauren says that, if she had known about the reality of job reentry, she would never have stayed home. Yet she also acknowledges that no other choice at the time would have been right. "I don't know how I would have managed if I were working when my children were young. At least, if I made mistakes as a mother, I was the one who made them."

EASING THE PRESSURE

Taking a time-limited leave can ease the financial and professional pressure that comes with "having it all" at the same time.

Dr. Janice Lowe's year off with her five-year-old and seven-year-old has been a kind of sabbatical for the whole family. Her husband, also a pediatrician, is on a one-year fellowship in Maryland, where the family has moved temporarily from their Massachusetts home. Janice is using the time to do research of her own. Everyone in the family has had a chance to experiment in new roles, without having to work around a timetable or deadline. Her children have been able to try new after-school activities without Janice worrying: How will I get them there? Will I get out of work on time?

Janice anticipated that the one-year move would be easier on their children if she were home. "Even my husband has commented on how nice it is. I think it has relieved stress from him—which actually wasn't one of my considerations. I was more concerned about the children. He used to do most of the cooking. Now I do it."

Although Janice would never consider staying at home for the long term (she would miss her patients too much), she has enjoyed the change of pace for the past year. She has no reservations about her upcoming return to her three-day-a-week schedule at one of Massachusetts General Hospital's community clinics. Her boss for the past seven years continues to support Janice's career choices. "She works longer hours and has more children than I, but she has never made me feel that

I should also work long hours. She is a real key to why I stay there."

MAKING IT WORK AT HOME

Being a full-time mother is not always rosy, particularly if a woman feels forced to choose between an unyielding profession and the demands of family life. How well her choice turns out may depend on whether she returned home burned out and disillusioned, or relaxed, confident, and at peace. Her husband's attitude toward her new role, and the level of parenting support he offers, can also make a huge difference in her adjustment to life without a salaried job.

Of the women we studied, the MBAs—more than the physicians or attorneys—underwent the most radical transformations in their life goals as they chose to leave the work force. Their stories sharpen the conclusion that the corporate world is the least forgiving and least accommodating to the needs of parents, even more so, surprisingly, than medicine. The MBAs in our survey said, with great conviction, that when they do return to work, they will never go back to the same situation they had left.

For many women who drop out, part-time work might have been the best option—if they had been able to find it. For example, Audrey Kadis discovered that the kind of part-time work available in business is a powerful disincentive to working part-time. In her case, after calculating take-home pay from a part-time job minus child-care expenses, no paycheck at all seemed a much less drastic financial option than she had originally thought.

We have interviewed many high-powered, career-motivated women who have quit the work force entirely, leaving behind years of valuable and hard-won experience. Their reasons for leaving often point to the clear need for realistic part-time solutions that will allow other women to remain in the work force, if that is their first choice.

Of course, no decision is perfect. Each woman, faced with a job-or-family choice, must do what she thinks is right. Audrey Kadis has reached some comfort in her choice.

"Some days I'm bored. Some days I'm isolated in the suburbs. Some days I'm afraid I'll never be able to 'work seriously' again. And some days I'm jealous of other women's success. But today my son and I took a 10-mile bike ride and hung out together. He's a great kid, and I know him better now than I did a year ago. You can't have it all."

What makes a woman who has devoted so much of her adult life to professional training decide to leave her work entirely? No single answer emerges, but many of the full-time mothers surveyed share common themes in their lives:

- **They feel that their lives have spun out of control.** They have learned to adjust their self-image and to judge self-worth by measures other than a career.

- **The stress of trying to make careers and children fit is simply not worth the personal toll on the family, on the marriage, and on themselves.**

- **The serious and prolonged illness of a child often presents no other choice than for one parent to leave the work force.**

- **Full-time work is not the answer.** Challenging part-time professional work would have been the first choice for many of these women, but it simply was not available. Leaving the work force is not without its costs— financially and in terms of career momentum.

- **More often than not, the work culture imposes an ultimatum: Continue your 60-hour week or we have no place for you.** Many women have experimented with part-time work but discovered that they have lost the excitement and reward that come with being part of the inner circle. They are not willing to trade time away from their children for a "job," rather than a career.

- **They feel a powerful maternal pull and want to spend more time with their children.** These women are certain they will enter the work force again, but many anticipate a significant career change when they do. They refuse to be bullied by how societal professional expectations and peer pressure say they should be leading their lives, using their degrees, using their professional credentials.

- **These families have been able to save enough money to rely on one income.** Professional women who leave the work force are often the first to admit that not every family has the financial resources to afford their lifestyle.

- **Many women want to give something back to the world, which has basically been very good to them, and are now serving as volunteers in their communities.** As Priscilla Vincent said, "Having had the opportunity to have both a career and a family—and feeling fortunate—I am glad I could do both and am happy I can now devote my energies to my family and my community. Not until I stopped 'working' was I able to repay any debt to the social structure around me."

CHAPTER SEVEN

◆ ◆ ◆

On the Home Front: Choose the Right Partner

For many women, progress in the office relies on change in the kitchen, figuratively and literally. The postfeminist generation of working women is facing a complex twist in the work/family dilemma. They are winning independence, self-reliance, and confidence in the workplace. However, to reach the personal and professional balance that eluded their mothers' generation, today's married women must be willing to rely on—and ask for—their husbands' support at home.

We were not supposed to write this chapter. Our editor suggested that we downplay the role of the husband and focus solely on the women's stories. Working women need support at home; the premise seems too basic to repeat. Yet, although we deliberately did not ask about the role of husbands as fathers, the women we surveyed told us anyway, in great detail. Their stories ranged from deep admiration for truly supportive husbands to profound disgust toward workaholic, uninvolved fathers.

"You can't have a real career without a supportive spouse," one talented feminist emphasized. "Make sure you choose your husband carefully," said another. And it goes both ways. Two solid careers can enhance a marriage. A 1992 *Working Mother* survey of 3,000 women revealed "that the more money a woman earns, the more likely she is to share the family's financial power and the happier the marriage."[1]

When a woman suddenly notices that she is doing everything her father did at work *and* everything her mother did at home, she finds herself discouraged and frustrated, and without a rational answer as to why men can still get away with not helping in the home.

Doesn't everyone at least *try* to choose the right partner? Our survey disclosed many couples who have found a workable balance between two busy careers and a shared family life. Yet just as many interviews revealed a huge gap between what *should* be happening and what really goes on at home. How do married couples reach a fair solution to the division of responsibilities? What are the consequences for the women who regret their choices or who realize that they have chosen the wrong partner?

As we studied the strains unique to working mothers, we found a wide range of definitions for contemporary family life, for both mothers and fathers. Some professional women specifically set out to marry men whose careers were less demanding than their own, but the majority married men who are also in fast-track careers. Many in this group reported unrelenting strain on the home front. The days are simply not long enough for these couples to devote the time they want to family life.

Happy, egalitarian marriages do exist. And women in these marriages admit that it takes hard work, the acceptance of some failures, and perpetual negotiation between two overburdened parents. No single solution will work for every couple. What may feel comfortable at one point will not work at another point in a career. One family's schedule may seem another family's nightmare. The most well-adjusted partners believe that their arrangements are fair, both for their individual and shared careers and for their family goals. The following stories present optimistic, though not always perfect, portraits of life on the home front for today's dual-career couple.

PARTNERSHIPS THAT WORK

Many husbands, no matter how involved with their children and how supportive of their wives' careers, often remain immune from most of the daily stresses that come with working and parenting. These men find it more comfortable to slip into the role they saw their own fathers play. Renee Matalon, an attorney for the Agency for International Development in Washington, D.C., married an exception to the traditional male.

Stephen Marcus is "the greatest and truest feminist I know," Renee says of her husband. "He shares completely in child care because he believes this is right and because he loves it!"

Both Renee and Stephen had mothers who worked outside the home. His mother ran a family-owned clothing store in Canada. Renee's mother worked as a secretary. "I didn't grow up thinking that a really good mother is home all the time; nor did my husband."

Renee's admiration for her husband is clear as she describes her marriage. "It is inconceivable to me to raise children, and enjoy it, and feel happy about it, without a man who believes that it is as much his job as a woman's."

Stephen was one of the few men at his 300-person law firm to take a paternity leave, using the two weeks allowed by company policy and adding a week of vacation time. Renee says, "I'm still startled by the number of men we know who say they don't feel comfortable with little tiny babies. Maybe the women reinforce this because they need to feel they're experts in something."

Although he is on a partnership track where evening and weekend work is taken for granted, Stephen's daily routine includes an early evening break to come home for dinner and to enjoy (and take responsibility for) his son Ezra's bath time—even if it means driving back to the office later to finish some work. If Stephen has to work on a Sunday, he has agreed with Renee that he will open his briefcase only during Ezra's naptime or bedtime.

Renee has slowed her own career a bit by working a four-day week, making motherhood her top priority as she prepares for the arrival of their second child. Work and family will always involve trade-offs and negotiations between Stephen and herself, she says. "We are definitely caught in the reality of his job and future partnership, but there has never been one moment when I've thought that parenting was more of my responsibility by default."

Renee Matalon advises young women to discuss their expectations about child-rearing even before they marry—then admits with a hearty laugh that she and Stephen became engaged three weeks after they met, without ever discussing how they planned to rear their children. Even during her pregnancy, neither of them worried about the other's commitment to real involvement in parenting. "I must have felt that children and family are innately important to Stephen."

And we found other instances of husbands who bucked tradition. For example:

• • •

MBA Christine Letts and her husband each took parental leaves when their two children were born. Christine took a 10-week maternity leave for each of her children, now aged five and eight. When she returned to her job in private industry, her husband began his parental leave: two months for their first child, and two weeks for their second.

When he took his first leave (an unpaid absence), Christine's husband was the first man in his corporation to do so. After their second child was born, he took only two weeks of vacation time because he knew that his boss was not as supportive this time around. He was considered unusual for taking time off to care for his children as infants, but has continued to receive raises and promotions at work. At home, each of his leaves helped set the tone for a genuine sharing of family responsibilities with Christine.

• • •

Lisa Churchville, MBA, class of 1979, and director of sales at an NBC affiliate, has a husband who moved with her from New York to Chicago when her career took off. After the advertising agency he joined in Chicago folded, he decided to go into the antiques business for himself.

When one of their children is ill, Lisa's husband does not have to ask permission to take a "sick-child day." On weekends, Lisa is the main parent, but during the week her husband is responsible for the household. "He takes care of the bill paying, the grocery shopping; on most days [he] waits for our caretaker to arrive in the morning, and comes home on time in the evening. This gives me more freedom at either end of the workday," Lisa says.

• • •

Fathers like these are more involved in life at home because they want to be, not because they have to be. Most couples with professional careers have enough income to pay for the best possible child care while they are at work. But who supervises the early morning, evening, and weekend routines? General "management" of parents' duties is often a key point of dispute: who makes the doctor's appointments, who finds emergency backup care, who remembers that cookies need to be baked for Scouts? This is where the real negotiation takes place.

THE MAN AT HOME

Of the 902 responses, only one househusband emerged in our survey. The doctor who married him knows he is unique, and took the time to type a detailed, single-spaced response solely about her mate.

Eileen Toth, MD, writes, "I have never met another professional woman whose husband's sole role was that of homemaker. Many women who say they are married to 'house-husbands' have spouses who are taking time off, temporarily, from their 'real' jobs, until their children are old enough for day care, school, or other alternatives."

Eileen's husband, Patrick Murto, has never worked outside of the home since their first child was born 14 years ago; their youngest child recently started first grade. She predicts that her husband will still be at home for years.

This physician has a "wife," and she readily admits that she could not do without him. "I never have to find child care if a child is ill and can't go to school. My 'baby-sitter' never calls in sick. The children are always at home with a parent, and they never arrive home from school to an empty house. There is always a fresh pot of coffee when I get home from work, and dinner is almost always prepared for me. These are things that most professional men with housewives take for granted, but I know very few working women who enjoy these privileges."

Because Eileen believes that no baby-sitter can establish the loving, secure, and stable environment that a parent can, live-in help was not an appealing choice for her. She can drive to work without the typical working mother worries about whether her children are being cared for by someone who shares her values about parenting.

She feels fulfilled by the nontraditional makeup of her family, yet she and her husband regularly encounter not-so-subtle prejudice toward and outright disbelief in their life-style. "The value of a professional woman is still judged by society in large part according to her husband's achievements and position," Eileen says.

"I know there are many people, even feminists, who think

it is at least 'odd' that a woman who graduated from medical school would be married to a man who never went to college and who doesn't have a 'job.' "

"Although most people can readily accept the idea of a doctor's wife who stays at home (even after the children are grown), and who is not as highly educated as her spouse, it is a different story for househusbands. Here is an example of a conversation I frequently have:

'Is your husband a doctor, too?'

'No, he's not.'

'Oh, what does he do?'

'He's a househusband. He stays at home and takes care of our children.'

'You mean he baby-sits?'

'Well, yes, and takes care of the house.'

'Oh, but what does he *really* do?' "

Termed a *baby-sitter*, Patrick Murto faces a new version of reverse discrimination and is accorded even lower status than "mother at home." Yet his family life is happy and well managed.

Despite her unusual support at home, Eileen Toth has made career sacrifices for her children and has chosen not to follow the model of the workaholic, never-say-no physician. She recently turned down the presidency of a county medical association simply because her time at home is so precious.

Because she is her family's sole source of income, she also must consider carefully how she spends her time. Although she was self-employed and able to set her own schedule by the time her second child was born, she found it financially disastrous to manage a four-month maternity leave without pay. Like the traditional father, she bears all the financial pressure to provide for her family.

Men married to women like Eileen Toth must have an exceptionally strong sense of self. In the Toth/Murto household, this is reinforced by the respect and admiration that Eileen holds for her husband—respect that most traditional wives have never been accorded. Such role switching also requires a confident woman, one who is secure enough to handle the comments from colleagues (mostly men with at-home wives), such as, "And why aren't you at home with your children?" Although stay-at-home fathers make up less than two percent of married parents, their numbers have risen from 61,000 in 1975 to 257,000 in 1990.[2]

The wife earns more than the husband in 18 percent of American households, a number expected to rise as more women move toward senior management.[3] An attorney in our survey who earns three times more than her husband views her own personal sacrifice as "giving over the 'mommy' role to my husband" for the sake of her career. She also realizes that she would not have become a law partner without him. "He leaves work on time, never travels, and covers all doctor appointments."

Are professional women saying that they essentially need "wives" at home because there is so little hope for real flexibility in the workplace? Or do they believe that a parent at home is the only solution to balancing careers and children? For many women, the answer to both questions is a partial yes. If they work in professions that offer no chance for flexibility, their only hope for a less-frenzied life is to rely on their husbands to do more than 50 percent at home. Their husbands' involvement also alleviates some of the guilt they may feel for not being home more: they do not have to rely exclusively on "buying" care for their children.

A WORD FOR THE MAN

Until recently there was no real catalyst for men to change. Society, the feminist movement and, to some extent, the professions have promoted new roles for women, but there has been far less momentum for men's roles to evolve. Women have been more prepared than their husbands for radical revolution in their expected roles.

Regardless of what he does at home, no man is entirely sure he is doing the right thing. Society still places little value on fathering. The accepted definition of "parenting" has been radically different for men and for women, although some fathers are trying to close the gap. These men, who are determined to participate fully in family life, face the same unyielding work culture that puts family behind, rather than beside, career.

This generation of men grew up with few questions and little cause for doubt. The role models provided by their own fathers and the senior men they met in their careers offered little incentive to change, mainly because these older men had never experienced the unresolved issues that dual-career couples must face. When today's men left home for college and graduate school, they were delighted to meet women who shared their interest in a profession but who also wanted a family. The combination seemed ideal.

What went wrong? While women's horizons for growth and change expanded, few men experienced any real pressure to broaden their roles. Why haven't men ever complained about not being able to have it all? Do they so readily accept the idea of putting profession ahead of family? Perhaps the role of primary breadwinner, plus the assumption that dedication to career equals lifelong job security, were enough to compensate for what they were missing in family time. Plus, of course, the most obvious reason: this is the way it always was.

Now that this unofficial contract has been broken, men are left to ponder whether professional "success" is worth the personal toll it exacts. A new vocabulary has arisen around the broadening of men's traditional roles: "full-time Dad," "Mr. Mom," even "Daddy Track."

At last the corporate world has begun to acknowledge that families exist for men as well as for women. *Fortune* magazine recently featured a cover story, "Why Grade 'A' Execs Get an 'F' as Parents," which focused on the unusually high incidence of drug abuse and other problems among children of executives. The article's bottom-line advice: "Spend time with the family." Other suggestions: "Tell your children you love them, especially when they are not anticipating such a comment. Nonverbal signs such as pats, hugs, kisses, and tousling their hair are also extremely important."[4]

The necessity of such obvious advice is a particularly sad commentary on the price men must pay for being single-minded fast-trackers in their careers.

MARRIAGES IN DISTRESS

The pace at which women are entering high-powered careers far exceeds the rate at which fathers are assuming equal parental duties. A Boston lawyer said, "It would be nice if someone asked men about *their* ability to combine careers and family. Women may be better able to do it, if 'success' includes satisfying relationships with family members."

A chief executive officer who holds an MBA and is the mother of twins describes her husband: "He is somewhat supportive, but he takes credit for being more supportive than he is—and expects a gold medal for being so." Although she is the family's primary breadwinner and brings home $300,000 a year more than her husband, she does most of the parenting. Not surprisingly, she is the one who feels the greatest stress between work and family.

Many of our respondents clearly recognized the distinction between "pitching in" with the children and assuming the emotional and psychological demands of being the primary parent. The balance between high-powered careers and family time is so tenuous for most couples that if parenting negotiations fall apart, the marriage itself may become vulnerable.

• • •

"My first marriage ended in divorce," said a corporate attorney. "I think a woman's relationship with her husband is the thing that suffers most when one tries to combine career and family."

• • •

A California litigator and mother of a toddler said, "My marriage ended due to my career success. But my daughter and my career have been wonderful."

• • •

Asked if she had been able to combine career and family successfully, a recently divorced city health director said, "I would like to think so but, admittedly, I was unable to be a doctor, mother, and wife simultaneously."

• • •

Marital strain can be an even greater problem for dual-career couples than the stresses they face as parents. Does a more demanding career automatically exempt a parent from duties on the home front? Can couples really take turns at being the primary parent? How does this inherent tension affect the children? These unresolved issues place a heavy burden on parental roles and can slowly kill a marriage.

Anger is the dominant emotion for women who come to realize that they are the primary parent, without choice and by default:

• • •

A psychiatrist married another medical doctor who was so supportive of her career that he took a second job to allow her to pursue an unpaid fellowship. Such devotion convinced her that he would offer the same emotional support when he became a father. She felt confident that she could enjoy a secure family life with him, as well as her demanding career.

Now divorced and a single parent to her three children, she observes, "I think that some women may be overly concerned about support for career development and not realize the importance of being with a man who demonstrates the capacities necessary for good fathering. Without a supportive spouse who is involved with the children, it becomes much more difficult to manage your career."

• • •

To the question, What would have made combining a family and career easier for you?, our respondents put "a more supportive husband" and "better child-care options" at the top of the list.

A Chicago lawyer, now divorced, is convinced by her own experience that "marital difficulties can be far more time-consuming and career-stressful than parenting demands." After making partner and having a child, she reduced her working hours for the sake of marital harmony, but her marriage failed anyway, her career stalled, and her self-respect shriveled.

Another lawyer, who has no children, commented, "I knew that marriage would require compromise. What I didn't know was how much of a career sacrifice would be required. If I had known, I might have postponed marriage even longer than I did."

Professional demands are difficult to refuse, and the rewards of parenting make it easy to devote every ounce of energy left at the end of the day to your children. The spouse seems to be the easiest to ignore.

• • •

A Seattle law partner and her husband, also a corporate lawyer, have recovered from a near divorce. When she was graduated from Harvard Law School, she believed she could have it all. As her feminist background "required," she first became partner, then had a child.

"At that point, my husband and I unconsciously put the marriage in third priority, behind careers and children," she said. The marriage weakened "and totally died after the second child. . . . We decided two years ago to work on the marriage and, if it didn't work, to divorce. The marriage has improved a great deal."

• • •

An administrative law judge, who completed law school after her children were in public school, is convinced that her career was the direct cause of her divorce. She knows that her children have benefited from having a working mother, but her husband was never able to accept her dual roles.

"Although he was verbally supportive of my decision to go to law school, he never was able to adjust his own life and attitudes so that he could assume some of the responsibilities I had always handled."

• • •

The judge's advice to dual-career families: Husbands, wives, and all family members old enough to participate must talk, constantly and deliberately, about plans, expectations, and frustrations.

THE TRADE-OFFS FOR WOMEN

Relocation for a career can tip the already shaky balance between profession and family. Women are the "trailing spouse" in 94 percent of job transfers for dual-career couples, according to a 1990 study in *Time* magazine.[5] Yet in the next 10 years, the number of women relocating for careers is expected to rise to nearly a quarter of all job transfers, the study predicts.

What trade-offs and/or sacrifices have women in our survey made to combine family and career?

A Boston law partner replied, "My marriage was sacrificed to my career in that I was not free to follow my husband in his career moves."

Many other women reported the jolt of discovering that their bosses, colleagues, and husbands expected a woman's career to be more dispensable than a man's.

An MBA management consultant from Virginia voiced her regrets: "Having had a taste of the responsibilities and excitement of the business world, I do sometimes resent having put my career well behind my husband's, just to hold the family together."

A medical doctor and mother of three young children said, "All child-related issues are my responsibility—not my husband's. My husband is a surgeon and shares none of the parenting burdens, although economically he gives me the freedom to hire excellent child-care people. Without his income, I would be much more limited."

Many women warned that marrying someone in the same profession is a big mistake. A physician from Ohio said, "Whatever you do, don't marry another doctor." A divorced MBA in New Mexico, who married a business school classmate, said, "Avoid—at all costs—marrying a man in the same profession."

A Kentucky attorney, whose first marriage to another Harvard Law School graduate ended in divorce, suggested, "Marry someone rich or someone who makes a lot of money working short hours. Avoid lawyers!"

EQUAL PARTNERS

One of the most content couples we surveyed has found ways to reach equality in each aspect of their lives.

Patricia Glowa, MD, and her husband are unusual in their marriage partnership: Each thinks the other is pulling an equal weight and no one is losing out on professional or family rewards. The couple practice medicine together; their children know their parents' roles are interchangeable.

The two physicians have an easy give-and-take at home, in part because their business partnership works so well. Together they provide a full-time family practice in rural New Hampshire and provide professional backup for each other in nearly every case (Patricia delivers babies; her husband does not). Each is in the office to see patients 2½ days a week. Patricia works at Planned Parenthood every other week; her husband teaches part-time at Dartmouth Medical School.

The couple have fine-tuned the details of working and parenting. The baby-sitter who greets the children after school also does the bulk of the housework. Whichever parent gets home first at night pitches in and takes care of the other household duties. Patricia and her husband have backup plans for contingencies, including clear agreement about child care for evenings at home. For example, if Patricia is at a school board meeting and her husband gets an emergency medical call, he beeps her at the meeting and she comes home immediately.

Like the Glowas, Sharon Tisher and her husband are interchangeable at home. Sharon Tisher is a trial attorney for a large Connecticut law firm. She works four days a week at 80-percent time. Seven years ago, when their first child was born, her husband also began working part-time. When Sharon had to be away for a two-month trial in Boston, her husband did all the parenting during the week.

Some women with full-time jobs also have managed to create a comfortable sharing of family responsibilities.

We asked Ann Fudge, MBA, director of marketing and

business development at General Foods, her secret for combining career and family successfully. Ann immediately answered, "I have a great husband," one who has been a key factor in her progress toward her corner office.

Unlike most of the women in our survey, Ann Fudge married her husband in college and had her two children, now teenagers, before she went to business school. Together she and her husband developed successful careers along with a happy family life. For example, when their children were younger, the couple negotiated who would pick them up at school (whoever worked closer) and who would stay home when a child was ill (the one who had the more flexible schedule that day).

Harvard Law School graduate Jan Sawyer* suggests, "Marry someone who wants to see you succeed and believes in equality—and who is willing and not too proud to do 50 percent of the child care."

For Jan's husband, the notion that only a woman can care for an infant is "preposterous." After their daughter was born, Jan took the first six weeks of parental leave; her husband Peter took the next.

Jan is an attorney with a government agency; Peter is a research scientist. They were married for 15 years before deciding to have a child. They agreed that neither could afford to take more than six weeks off, but that each wanted to take some time to enjoy their newborn. Their colleagues' reactions at work were tactless and negative.

"Boy, is Peter unlucky to be married to you!" several men told Jan. The women were no kinder when they asked, "Aren't you upset about returning to work so soon?" or "Why did you stop breast-feeding so soon?" Peter's fellow scientists basically told him he was a "wimp" for staying at home and training the nanny.

Jan is fully aware that her husband is an exception. For example, he gets home first to feed and bathe their three-

*An asterisk after a name designates a pseudonym.

month-old. "Our friends' seemingly egalitarian relationships seem to fall apart as soon as their children are born," Jan said. She and her husband both feel the strain between profession and family, but "at least we're exhausted together. I don't come home tired to a man who's sitting down, reading the paper."

Jan is convinced that women, too, are responsible when inequality exists in the home. Many women, she says, are simply not bold enough to ask for help. For many of those who do, their husbands can come up with endless reasons to not pitch in: their higher incomes, teasing from colleagues, better parental leaves for women, men's inability to nurse an infant.

Jan is being considered for a federal judgeship and says, "My husband has enabled me to do something my colleagues thought only men could do." Until men do their share at home, she knows that women will never be on a level playing field in their professions.

NEW ROLES FOR WOMEN AND MEN

Women in our survey are trying to make sense of the new roles for husbands and wives, as parents and as professionals. Their advice may make the transition easier for other couples:

- **Do whatever is best for you and your family.** Others may be judgmental, but there is no single right way for a marriage to function. The details of your choice are less important than how comfortable you both feel with the way you divide parental responsibilities in your home.

- **Clarify what you really want from family and career.** If you don't feel comfortable delegating most of the child care to a third person, you or your husband will have to sacrifice career momentum at some point in your child's life.

- **If possible, before you marry, and certainly before you have children, define household and child-care responsibilities.** Make sure you both understand the other's willingness to assume parental duties.

- **Consider how the demands of your career will affect your ability to fulfill your roles at home.** Evaluate the amount of travel required, the frequency of emergency meetings, the necessity for evening and weekend work, the predictability of work schedule, and your financial resources to pay for the high cost of child care.

- **Plan ahead financially for the arrival of your children.** Even high-salary couples feel the financial strains of parenting. Reliable child care and other support for working parents becomes a huge component of what it costs to raise a child.

- **Determine what type of child care will best meet your needs for both your career and your life at home and recognize that these needs will change at different stages of your child's development.**

- **Decide which household tasks you can contract out, particularly if both you and your spouse choose to remain in fast-track careers.** Contract work may include housecleaning, cooking, grocery delivery, driving children to after-school activities.

- **Negotiate with your partner from a position of strength.** First determine your common values and expectations for family life. Men whose own mothers have worked outside the home are more likely to support their wives in dual roles.

- **Agree that both parents will have certain responsibilities, even if one is working more hours than the** other. Shared parenting is positive for both the children and the marriage.

- **Remember that negotiated decisions can change.** Leave room for reexamination, renegotiation, and trade-offs in your expectations.

- **Be courageous and flexible in your decisions about nontraditional and experimental strategies for your marriage and family life.** Fairness—and perceptions about fairness—is more critical to family harmony than any absolute measures of division in roles, as you are blazing new paths for the next generation.

CHAPTER EIGHT

◆ ◆ ◆

The Hungry God
of Success

Vacation packing list: beach clothes, sunblock, paperback novel, Fax machine. Fax machine? Always on call!

PAYING THE PIPER

The hungry god of success is not easily satisfied.[1] Rigid and relentless, she is unyielding in the price she extracts from those who follow the path toward the top. It is hardly surprising that *fatigue* and *stress* are the two words that female MBAs, lawyers, and physicians use most frequently to describe their lives.

Most career women today, not just mothers, share the dilemma of how to reconcile their personal values with the rituals of success that their professions impose: long hours, face time (the time one is visibly present in the office), and total availability. The 902 women in our survey want to feel good about themselves as mothers and professionals but instead many feel sad, disappointed, angry, and frustrated because each role competes so fiercely for their time and energy. The respondents were unanimous in seeing virtually no change in a work culture that is still based on male professionals with wives at home. A computer company executive told us, as many women did, that her boss treated family life as a weakness and said to her, "I had children, but my wife made sure they didn't interfere with *my* work."

One-third of the women who responded to our survey do not have children, yet many of them also have reluctantly concluded that the price of conforming to the traditional male rules of the game may be far too high.

A lawyer, who works in her office at least three nights a week and on most weekends, says her career has dictated her decision about whether to marry. "It's hard to find someone who understands the demands of my job." She cautions future lawyers about the choices she believes they will have to make between professional and personal life.

"Think very hard about what you want to do. Don't just default into a job and think you can make changes later. Once your ego gets involved and you invest your time and energy, it's very hard to put that aside or step down."

Long-term, unquestioned loyalty to a single organization is rare in today's professional world—and for good reason. Women and men are seeing repeated examples of downsizing, during which even the most intense commitment, burning dedication, and outstanding performance no longer guarantee job security. Also, as they move closer to the top, younger fast-trackers meet senior professionals, mostly men, who regret their own failed marriages and strained relationships with grown children. This generation of professionals has begun to worry that they will be victims of that same fate unless they rethink the kind of lives they are leading.

The payoffs for the 90-hour week are beginning to pale for many women, and for some men as well. As committed as they are to their jobs, they realize that a fat salary no longer compensates for having to jam an entire home life into an hour or two each weeknight. Time is the most precious commodity for today's professionals.

Until recently, women were willing, and expected, to do all the accommodating when work and family choices conflicted. To satisfy the hungry god of success, these female managers, lawyers, and physicians often made painful personal sacrifices—giving up or delaying having a family—only to learn that, even though they played the game by male rules, they were the wrong sex to become full-fledged members of "the team."

The issue of gender becomes more critical as we look toward the workplace of the future. Demographic trends of the 1990s project that women will make up two-thirds of the new entrants into the work force in the next decade. Of this group, 75 percent will bear at least one child, thus permanently changing the character of work in every profession. Yet many senior executives still act as if these "women's issues" will either just go away or remain on the periphery of the "real" issues. The cultural barriers to change appear so deep and so powerful that today's professional women worry that life at work will be no different for their own children's generation.

Opening the door to let women into the professions was not enough. The first generation of professional women did not dare to challenge the hungry god, because they knew their positions were shaky at best. Today's generation expects more. These women are beginning to prove that there is more than one way to get a job done. They are looking for a new definition of "success," a definition that includes the home front.

THE STATUS OF WOMEN TODAY

Where do working mothers stand today? What do they need to move forward? Despite the paper trail of "family-friendly" policies, the professions have made little headway toward a family-friendly work culture. Such policies remain, for the most part, promises of what *could* and should be.

A mother of two and an international trade lawyer describes it like this, "It's like a barren land out there. It's a lonely road."

The Glass Ceiling

Many women have discovered that there is not only a glass ceiling in business but a glass locker room as well. They can see what's going on from a distance, but they can never fully participate in the deals cut on the golf course, in the gym, and over a glass of beer after work. This unwritten work culture, the behind-the-scenes political maneuvering and positioning for power, remains inaccessible to most women.

The "technical" barriers to women's progress have been down for years. Women have proven, in every profession, that their gene pool offers all the intellect and talent necessary to do the job. Why, then, are they still held back?

First, many men are not even discreet about exhibiting sexist behavior. The number of men who still refuse to accept women as equals signals a serious and sustained challenge to the feminist movement. Also, the Old Boy network, and a flourishing younger version, are alive and well. While their rules may not necessarily be designed to be exclusive, female lawyers, doctors, and managers learn quickly that they can play only if they accept the fact that work clearly comes first, and home, a distant second.

Our survey asked women if they felt that they have paid a price in their careers for having children. A senior investment banker answered, "I paid a price for being *female*."

Seventy percent of the 400 women executives queried in a 1992 *Business Week*/Harris Poll said they view "the male-dominated corporate culture" as a barrier to their success. The same poll indicated that 57 percent of the women believe that "the rate of progress for corporate women has slowed down or stopped altogether."[2]

An MBA, and mother of three, returned to a full-time schedule as an investment banker after each maternity leave, but finally concluded that the glass ceiling was unbreakable, and not worth the sacrifice.

"One reason I gave up work was that I wasn't being paid what a man would earn and didn't get the advancement opportunities a man would have. I had a very satisfying job, in content and prestige, but the really lucrative jobs probably weren't open to me. So the personal sacrifice didn't seem worthwhile. I am much happier now, as are my husband and children."

Only 2 percent of senior executives are women. In law, 94 percent of partners are men, and "women partners are increasing by only about 1 percent a year."[3] The glass ceiling has remarkably few cracks, despite the number of talented women who have entered the traditional male-dominated professions of business, law, and medicine. One ready explanation is that women have not been in these professions *long* enough to fill more than a tiny percentage of top positions. A 1992 *Fortune* feature on executive women included a poll of 201 chief executive officers (CEOs) and reported that only 18 percent of those surveyed believe it is "very likely" that in the next 20 years a woman will be selected to run their businesses. "Why? The CEOs . . . cite a host of reasons, but the biggest barrier, a few of them admit, is an irrational one—plain and simple discrimination."[4] The reality is that very little has changed since the glass ceiling was constructed.

The Maternal Wall

Working mothers face an extra barrier to landing the plum assignments and keeping their careers on the same fast track as that of their male colleagues. We call this powerful impediment the maternal wall. Women may fail to recognize its existence until it is too late to figure out how to climb over or around it. Often camouflaged by family-friendly policy statements, the wall is invisible and unyielding, yet women find it difficult to prove they have run into it. Many do not realize how destructive the maternal wall will be to their careers until they have actually hit it. For example:

- A female physician hits the maternal wall when she learns it's OK for a man to refuse weekend coverage so he can attend a football game but it's not OK for her to sign out to attend her son's birthday party.

- A qualified woman discovers the maternal wall when she is passed over for promotion after she becomes a mother, even though she took no maternity leave and has the best credentials for the job.

- A law partner hits the maternal wall when a senior partner and long-time mentor suddenly drops her from the good cases as soon as she announces her pregnancy.

When a man leaves a meeting early to pick up his child, he is often praised as the new breed of father: sensitive, involved, caring, and fair-minded. When a woman does the same thing, she is often called unprofessional, uncommitted, or "not management material."

Women who have chosen to follow traditional male career paths and play by men's rules still advise other women, "Have your children at one job and your career at another." In other words, hide the fact that you are a mother, because motherhood is bound to be used against you.

A lawyer, working her way up the partnership track, is discouraged about how to find time for her family. "Basically, women must choose one or the other. There is no such thing as 'balance' because it's impossible to succeed in a law firm without being totally committed."

Even in organizations in which forward-looking executives have mandated "family-friendly" policies, the real rules often dictate that a woman will be passed over for promotion if she tries to use those policies, particularly when everyone else is working long hours. "Men don't understand the conflicts, and most older women are bitter about the sacrifices they have had to make—and take it out on the younger ones," said an attorney.

Men with stay-at-home wives don't have to put in a "second shift" at home.[5] The home shift, the second shift, remains a woman's domain and is often the point of conflict between wife and husband. The division of roles at home—by gender—tends to fortify the maternal wall at the office. When men do not function as equal parents in the home, they cannot fully understand the double-shift syndrome and therefore have little personal incentive to offer creative work/family initiatives in the office.

A professor of law, married to another academic who is a "very involved" father, said, "We've hardly begun to make the fundamental changes needed to assure that all parents can be living forces in their kids' lives. Too many of my male contemporaries are nearly as marginal in their children's lives as were their fathers."

There has been little visible momentum toward a work culture that is more accepting of parents, and particularly of women as mothers. In fact, the fields of business, law, and medicine seem to have taken a few steps backward, now that there are enough women in each profession to satisfy affirmative action requirements and to stifle any charges of broad-scale discrimination.

Barbara Pearce, a self-employed real estate developer and Harvard MBA, explained why she and her husband decided that he should be the one to take their son with him when they each had an evening meeting. "Usually my husband took him, on the theory that people would think he was a real prince, but they would think I was disorganized. They believe that women who can't get child care don't plan very well, whereas men who bring their children are really committed fathers."

Barbara knows firsthand how natural it is to worry about

what people will think of your work ethic. When her first child was born on a Friday, she felt compelled to return to her office the following Monday. "I had only been in the business a couple of years and wanted people to think I was serious about working."

Even if a woman's only maternity-related request is for a brief leave after her baby's birth, she may encounter discrimination because she is a mother. Bosses and colleagues may feel they cannot count on her anymore; they may write her off for promotions; or they may give her a hard time because she has chosen a personal life so different from their own. For instance:

• • •

A partner in a major New York law firm has discovered that, since she became a mother eight months ago, "the senior partners treat me as dead." This discrimination, which she knows will affect her future assignments and promotions, has kindled an anger for which she has no professional recourse.

• • •

A physician at a major Boston hospital feels backed into a corner by arbitrary professional obligations. Even though she sees patients beginning at 6:00 A.M., she is still required to attend meetings scheduled after her 12-hour day and 6:30 P.M. departure time, when she needs to relieve her baby-sitter. "Any deviation from accepted practice stands out, requires explanation, causes resentment, and interferes with the male environment's tunnel vision."

• • •

What types of parental behavior are detrimental to a woman's career? Our 902 respondents said that nearly *all* demonstrations of parental duties—except taking a maternity leave of six weeks or less—have a negative effect on a woman's career. Basically, any time a mother at work exhibits parental behavior different from a man's, she risks adding another brick to her own maternal wall.

An MBA banker, sad and bitter about how her image changed following a three-month maternity leave, said, "That's not what people expect from a dedicated, high-performing employee. They want your soul."

Here lies the dilemma: how do you split a soul in two?

THE WRITTEN VERSUS THE UNWRITTEN RULES

Organizations typically operate with two sets of rules: (1) the rules on paper that technically define conditions of employment, and (2) the unwritten standards of behavior that clearly must be followed if you want to be taken seriously and become a member of "the team."

Personnel manuals and summaries of benefits rarely present a realistic picture of how an organization actually works. It is a rare corporation, law firm, or hospital that has genuinely evolved toward real acceptance of maternity leaves and genuine accommodation of family needs. Examples abound:

• • •

> When a Boston physician took a one-month paid maternity leave and two months of unpaid time, she overheard a colleague whisper loudly enough for her to hear, "She's sure milking the system for all it's worth." Ironically, the other physicians who agreed with the comment had each encouraged their own wives to stay at home when their children were young.

• • •

An MBA computer whiz, and recent adoptive mother of a Romanian baby, says she cannot even consider telling her boss she does not want to travel for a while. "It's considered weakness. He attacks!" Like many women, she reluctantly admits, "People in personnel talk supportively, but the reality is that everyone wants things as they were."

• • •

A highly paid investment banker, and mother of three, says, "My maternity leaves were less than the firm allowed, so they were deemed OK. Women who have taken the maximum leave have been perceived as undedicated to the firm. A reduced workweek is viewed as leaning on one's colleagues." She has also noticed that bonuses, which are supposed to be based on financial results, are in reality largely determined by face time in the office.

Face Time

The intense value placed on face time, that is, the time one is visibly present in the office, is the greatest barrier to a more comfortable alliance between professional ambition and a satisfying family life. The more face time—the more hours, evenings, and weekends—the more points. It is a ritual firmly embedded in the work culture and rarely challenged.

The face-time ritual deducts points for the woman who comes in at 7:00 A.M. so she can pick up her child at the day-care center by 6:00 P.M. It adds points for the man who comes in at 9:00 A.M. and stays at his desk until 8:00 P.M. After-hours face time yields the highest points of all.

An MBA and former buyer for a major New York chain, now a mother of three, says, "The expected behavior was to be in the store on the weekends, whether or not your business required it."

Face time is why people lie about leaving early to take a child to a doctor, even if they leave the office with a briefcase full of work. Face time also explains why many women feel the need, professionally, to keep their maternity leaves as short as possible. One survey respondent's comment was typical: "My two-month leave wasn't long enough, but I felt I *had* to get back to work."

The concept of face time tends to hit part-timers the hardest. People will overlook an absence from the office because of travel, and being in a meeting is always a good excuse for not returning telephone calls the same day. However, no one forgets when a part-timer cannot be reached at 5:00 P.M. because she has left at 4:00 P.M.

IMPEDIMENTS TO PROGRESS

Organizations cannot completely ignore the fact that more and more working women are working mothers. Heeding the demographics, slick corporate publications are beginning to appear, touting the "family-friendly" nature of their company. Articles in publications ranging from *Woman's Day* to *The Wall Street Journal* tell us what needs to be done to mediate the work/family standoff. What, then, is standing in the way of real progress for working parents?

The following assumptions must fall before any real and lasting change in the work culture can occur:

1. Career commitment means the family must come in a distant second.

2. Face time is the best measure of dedication.

3. "Real" professional work can only be done full-time.

4. A job with any significant level of responsibility must always override a personal life.

5. Women are the only ones who care about family.

So why is it taking so long to get rid of these notions? There are several reasons:

- Women have been reluctant to admit publicly that they have been made to feel that their careers and their children are on a collision course. Their initial, automatic and mistaken reaction was to believe that *they* must be doing something wrong if their family and work lives were precariously out of balance.

- Basically, no one likes to change. For most CEOs, law firm partners, and senior physicians, there is no immediate incentive to do things differently. Yet in the next decade, the economy will be increasingly dependent on working mothers who may require some, however minimal, accommodation for parenting.

- The mistaken assumption persists that men *have* to work and women do not.

- Regardless of what is on paper, the *real* rules of a work culture often penalize women who dare to take advantage of family-friendly policies.

- The stress of economic necessity in virtually every facet of the work force has stifled many of the voices that would like to speak up for change. The last thing people concerned about job security will demand is flexibility.

- Innovation requires a period of experimentation, including the provision for some failures. However, serious global competition seems to have tempered the climate for risk of any sort.

While professionals may still be averse to openly fighting the traditional team rules, that does not mean they intend to follow the same rules forever. As Walter Kiechel III suggests in a recent article, "When the recovery comes, expect not fissures in the workaholic ethics but gaping chasms."[6] In her book *The Overworked American*, Juliet B. Schor describes the time squeeze imposed on women and men who are now working an extra month each year compared with 20 years ago. As Schor points out, for the first time in 15 years people rate leisure as "more important" than their work.[7]

SEIZING THE SOUL

Business, law, and medicine no longer lure and seduce the soul as they once did. The most significant change for professional women has been in their attitudes about the meaning of work in their lives. They simply refuse to buy into the notion that professional reward comes only in one package. Asked if they have been able to combine career and family successfully, few of our respondents offered an unqualified yes or no. Many said they suffer at least some doubt about whether they have made the best choices for each of their roles.

A Vermont doctor and mother of three says, "I'm always tired. I live in high gear trying to get it all done. You can have two of three things: family, career, sanity. Take your pick."

Typical were comments such as, "It depends on what day you ask me," or "I'll have to wait to see how my children turn out."

When virtually everyone in the work force had the same family structure—Dad at work, Mom at home—the world was cleanly divided. That model is fading fast. Dual-career couples, single parents, and at-home fathers now challenge traditions about choices between work and home.

In a study of work-family boundaries, Douglas Hall and

Judith Richter identify gender differences in the degree of stress that managers feel as they move between profession and family.

> *"The men tended to leave the office later than the women; they were also more likely than their wives to go through an unwinding period (reading the newspaper, for example) before getting fully involved in their home activities. Thus, men experienced more flexible boundaries than women, both at work and at home."*[8]

Traditionally, men and women have been discouraged from talking about family life in the office but have been encouraged to let work spill over into the home. Many professional women have decided that the degree to which work encroaches upon their family time is dramatically out of proportion and fully out of control. Power breakfasts, evening conferences, home fax machines, and weekend business travel are clear signs of how little is left of private time in the home.

Physicians, more frequently than either the lawyers or businesswomen that we surveyed, commented on the declining status of their profession. Many now question whether their rigorous training and the continuing stress of long, unpredictable hours are worth the high degree of personal sacrifice.

One physician put it this way: "The MD track ain't what it used to be. Before, at least you had job satisfaction, money, and power. Now the money is gone, and everyone tells you how to do your job. It's too frustrating. I might as well have a job that I can forget when I leave."

A Boston physician has geared down from a 75-hour workweek doing cancer research to a 50-hour workweek in industry. Before her marriage, she described her career as "my whole life." Today, as a mother of a toddler, she says, "Had I realized earlier how difficult this job/marriage/mother triad was to balance, I might have made different career decisions—chosen a medical specialty with fewer demands and greater flexibility."

Women have discovered that it does not matter how much they are willing to give up in salary and professional prestige in order to spend time with their children. The balance of trade-offs between work and family is always tipped in favor of the office.

An assistant professor of medicine and the mother of two, who regularly puts in 80-hour weeks, has given up personal hobbies, lunch breaks, and all adult friendships, yet she still believes she has paid a price in her career for having had children. "If I had put in more hours, I'd be further ahead now."

The rewards of parenting far exceed her career sacrifices, she says, but she remains disappointed that no one at work seems to understand her dilemma as a mother. She did not dare even request a maternity leave for the birth of either of her children, having reluctantly accepted a work ethic that denies the existence of family life.

A psychiatrist and mother of two children geared her practice down to 25 hours a week. Her patients were unconcerned, but her colleagues expressed utter disbelief. "I generally do not look to my work environment for support," she said. "I only expect a lack of any intervention. Everyone is openly, verbally supportive. The resistance is subtle. I find that non-MDs are among the most supportive. As a physician, I have departed from the norm of long hours and workaholism. There is pressure to conform. Our current practice manager (single, no kids, age 40, workaholic) even tried to discourage me from joining the group."

Many women in our survey confirmed that their early definition of success, which was fostered by their prestigious graduate training and fine-tuned during their professional lives, simply does not work for them anymore. Given a shaky economy, corporate takeovers, and the relatively new phenomenon of professionals losing their jobs, people are thinking more deeply about how they are spending—or not spending—their days.

Like so many highly trained women, MBA Sue Sheffler needed time to separate what her credentials "told" her she should be doing in the workplace from what she really wanted to do. Once she untangled her own myths about success, she determined that balancing a career and family simply meant doing what is right for her. In hindsight, Sue reflects that more balanced training at the Harvard Business School would have made combining profession and family easier for her. "It's a boot camp and leads to the illusion that career should be primary in life."

Sue discovered, particularly after the birth of her second child, that she had nothing left emotionally to give to her children at the end of the day. For now, she has taken herself off the fast track to work a regular 40-hour week as the health products director for a major insurance company. The relatively small salary cut she took, to reduce her hours by at least 15 percent, was worth the price. "Quality of life for me means being alert enough to just 'be' sometimes with each of my children—the opposite skill of being a good manager."

Sue Sheffler was not the only one.

• • •

A former 90-hour-a-week MBA marketing executive recounted what prompted her to give up a fat salary, company car, garage in New York City, and 100,000 miles a year of frequent flying. "Two months before I left the marketing arena, I refused to go dancing with clients after a business dinner because I was scheduled to do an 8:00 A.M. strategy presentation. When I returned to my office a few days later, I had a written reprimand in my file waiting for me." Even without the demands of marriage and children, this MBA decided to gear down to a 45-hour-a-week management job "for reasons of personal sanity."

• • •

A feisty investment manager, married but not planning to have children, advises younger colleagues, "Don't buy into the macho assertion that anybody who doesn't work 60 hours a week isn't serious or can't excel. Anyone who can't avoid the time-wasting B.S. and do a top-level professional job in 40 hours a week is *dumb*! It ain't that hard, ladies. The pretense that it is, is some kind of primate territorial display, or something."

While this view of work may seem extreme, it questions the basic assumption that time on the job always measures productivity.

• • •

A New York pediatrician and mother of a toddler says, "I think I long ago worked 'ambition' out of my system so that I mostly don't need to climb the male 'Harvard' ladder to feel personally and professionally fulfilled."

This busy physician works a full-time clinical schedule of 50 hours a week. She recognizes, however, that most of her medical school colleagues work an even heavier pace. "I think if I had accepted the goals I was taught at Harvard Medical School—aggressive ambition, competitiveness, workaholic approval—then it would be much harder to mix family and career. Until men and women let go of that professional model of success, neither will be able to merge family and career effectively."

• • •

Among 902 responses, we received one vividly dissenting opinion on career versus family from a single, 36-year-old lawyer:

"My couples' counselor told me that a lover, even a spouse, comes and goes, but a career is always there. *So* if one has to err on one side or the other . . . ."

This generation of working mothers has observed closely what has happened to the previous generation, and they are often discouraged by what they see.

An MBA from Virginia says that too many people think that what they are is their job. " 'Careers' are highly overrated. The term *career* carries a baggage of ideas, conjures up images of sacrificing outside interests, working long hours, of identities totally wrapped up in a job (you are what you do), relentlessly climbing the ladder to the top."

Most lawyers find it virtually impossible to meet the criteria for partnership with anything less than a standard, breakneck pace for seven years. A few law firms in Boston and Washington, D.C., have begun to offer on-site evening and weekend child care, allowing parents to expand even further their billable hours with the unfortunate side effect of children who can now spend seven days a week in day care. This extended day-care concept is an example of seemingly good corporate practice taken to extremes.

● ● ●

Karen Munroe,* a lawyer and mother of three, began as an associate at a traditional Boston law firm, where the life-style of the sole female partner "showed me the cost of sacrificing self and family." A Princeton and Harvard Law School graduate, Karen now works as an attorney for a medical center in Colorado. "I have limited my ambitions in my profession as my ambition to strengthen my family has grown," she says.

Karen has discovered that the health care industry, already dependent on female labor, has had no choice

*An asterisk after a name designates a pseudonym.

but to accommodate parents in the workplace. Her professional trade-offs include a lower salary and less prestige than she had in the law firm. Nevertheless, "I still love it and wouldn't trade it for anything, but I imagine my law school classmates would rank my position low on the totem pole."

• • •

Diane Nygaard, a lawyer and mother of twin boys, has concluded, "What is detrimental to a woman's career is to work in a male institution." Now successfully self-employed, she described the job she left behind. "I was the only female partner in the law firm, and I remember being told I should be in the office watching football on TV with my partners every Saturday because 'that's when the politicking occurred'. . . . In terms of money, I've actually made more money in my own practice, worked on more interesting cases, and been able to control my hours to maximize time with my husband and children."

Diane has expanded her practice to include two other attorneys. "We attempt to maintain a collegial atmosphere and describe ourselves as a 'new age' law firm. I will only hire people who are interested in making their practice *part* of their lives and not the totality of their lives." The best advice she ever received, she says, was to "forget I went to Harvard Law School. This has allowed me to consider options that have made me happier."

• • •

These women have figured out that the values touted in the workplace have never been in harmony with the basic desire for a satisfying family life. For too long, men, as well as women, have missed out on the fundamental rewards of parenting because they have not been allowed any other way to have a "successful" profession than to work all the time.

This postfeminist generation of professional women is just beginning to propose that work can still be satisfying, even if a career pace or work schedule is nontraditional. Their individual experiments will advance real and collective solutions to the "great divide" between work and family.

A FAMILY-FRIENDLY REALITY: LESSONS FOR THE WISE EMPLOYER

The person at the top of an organization can play a key role in assuring that women's careers are not derailed when they bear a child or assume other family responsibilities. Two examples illustrate the difference one powerful person can make in shaping a work culture:

• • •

At the StrideRite Corporation in Boston, full credit for an innovative center, which combines child care and care for the elderly, goes to former StrideRite Chairman of the Board Arnold Hiatt.

• • •

NCNB Bank in Charlotte, North Carolina, is repeatedly singled out for its progressive policies toward flexible work arrangements. The bank's commitment to change begins with its chairman, Hugh McColl, a now-involved father of three, who still suffers regrets for missing his son's championship basketball game. McColl was at a bank convention when his son's team lost the big game by two points.[9]

• • •

Do women stop caring about a career when they have a baby? Does commitment to a career falter because of the demands of parenting? Must career and children be on a collision course? Is it *really* in a company's best interest to treat working mothers well? The case of Paramount Pictures executive Cecelia Andrews suggests a firm answer of no to the first three questions and a resounding yes to the last. Her story demonstrates that a "flexible" employer does not have to lower its expectations for employee performance. Instead, each side must be motivated to work in a partnership involving give-and-take and clear communication.

Cecelia Andrews, a single parent of a teenage daughter, has stayed with Paramount Pictures since 1974, mainly because of the work environment. "I have been extremely happy at Paramount. However, . . . one of the reasons I have remained here for 16 years has been my daughter. I could have changed companies several times, but . . . a major factor in my not leaving is that Paramount has been supportive of my parenting. I know that in the early years of my career, I could have made a better salary by changing companies, but my ability to parent within the context of my career was always a more important consideration for me."

Because of her promotions, Cecelia found that her 50-hour workweeks actually expanded after her daughter was born, yet she has always felt comfortable asking to juggle her hours occasionally. Instead of taking a traditional block of vacation time, she spread out her time one summer by taking every Friday off for three-day weekends with her daughter. Another year she took her vacation time by leaving at 2:30 P.M. each day to arrive home in time to greet her daughter's camp bus.

These simple and reasonable examples of flexibility have been a major factor in Cecelia's loyalty to Paramount. She adds that her seniority and proven track record made it easier for her employer to accommodate her need for family time. Cecelia was free to do both her jobs—executive and mother—without guilt on the home front or fear of a reprimand at work.

"Some of the flexibility that I have had at work has been a direct result of my having positions of greater responsibility that are less supervised. As I have moved 'up the ladder,' there have been fewer people that I am responsible to, and this has made it easier for me to direct how I will do my work: coming in early and not staying late, or taking time off in the middle of the day to volunteer at my child's school, and then coming back to work late."

As important as what her employer did do was what it did not do, Cecelia says. Paramount did not make her feel guilty for being a parent. They did not stop grooming and promoting her because of a maternity leave and an occasional day off to tend a sick child. No one told her that it was wrong to attend a special school event during the workday. No one pitted her maternal instincts against her professional pride. In return, Cecelia offers an intense loyalty to her employer—rare by today's standards—as she continues to move up the executive track, perhaps a little slower than her Harvard training mandated, but still at a steady professional pace.

Susan Baronoff made a conscious decision to take more control over her work schedule when her first child was born. Since becoming partner in a medium-size Boston law firm, Susan has worked hours ranging from 20 to 70 a week. "I returned part-time for about six months after each maternity leave. Then when Laura, my oldest, went from day care into elementary school, I felt it would be a big transition for her and that staying for the after-school program each day would be too much. I arranged to come home early two days a week. I did that for a year and it was good for her."

Susan has achieved a work/family balance unusual for most lawyers and tells us that she can leave her office most days at 5:30 P.M., with some catching up in the evening one or two days a week. "I think our firm is unusual in that we have a fair number of women attorneys—7 of 23 partners are women. And it's acceptable in our firm to work 'normal hours.' "

As we interview Susan over the telephone while her children are home with the flu, she talks about how critical it is to have some flexibility at the margin. This flexibility has meant some trade-offs professionally, which Susan believes are reasonable to expect. She has missed out on a few exciting cases that would have required significant travel, including a recent trip to Greece involving representation of a bank.

"I probably have developed less quickly as a trial lawyer because I have not sought heavy trial work since having children. I feel I have to hold the line at this particular time of my life." At the same time, Susan is able to volunteer in her daughter's classroom and to attend special events held during the school day.

Her advice to other mothers? "Decide what's good for you and your family. Don't try to fit other people's models of the 'proper' balance."

Women like Cecelia Andrews and Susan Baronoff have discovered the keys to professional satisfaction without having to give up the rewards of a personal life. Their employers—even those willing to grant only a small margin of flexibility—are benefiting from the skills of these talented and productive women.

There is no foundation for the fear that women of childbearing age are a risky investment for company resources and training. *Working Woman* recently reported:

> *"Only about 14 percent of new mothers do not go back to work at the end of their maternity leaves, and nearly two-thirds return within three months of giving birth. . . . Women with supportive supervisors come back even faster and in greater numbers."*[10]

Only 15 percent of U.S. households reflect the traditional, nuclear family: an employed husband, homemaker wife, and children.[11] Few families have the luxury of an extended family to help with child care; in fact, many parents of young children also care for elderly parents. Yet few institutions have kept pace with the new and rapidly evolving demographics of the work force.

Nearly 40 percent of the women we surveyed have changed jobs because of family responsibilities. If professional women find no reasonable accommodation for parenting in their jobs, they will try to go elsewhere, and their organization's investment in them will be lost, and gained by a more supportive company.

An assistant professor of medicine, who felt pressured not to take a maternity leave for either of her children, summarized the conditions that must change. "All my work contacts act as if one's family and work are totally separate worlds."

A 1991 report by the Boston Bar Association deserves credit for its humane tone in recognizing "the importance of bonding between both parents and infant."[12] The report also recognizes the practical economic factors that determine how much employers should bend to accommodate family needs. The report makes one basic recommendation: An employee should establish some kind of a track record in time and ability before asking for flexibility. The report suggests, for instance, that lawyers looking toward a part-time schedule should first work two years full-time in their professional specialty.

Corporate-sponsored child care by itself will not eliminate work/family stress. The women we surveyed can afford high-quality child care. For them, the dilemma centers on priorities and finding a work environment that recognizes the importance of their other role as parent.

Employers must consider new criteria for "success." Time in the office can no longer be the sole measure of productivity. If employers are having trouble with the concept of part-time work and its resultant reduction in face time, will they be able to handle the advanced notion of "flexplace" and the likelihood of telecommunication from the home? Rather than focusing on traditional, often subjective, measures of commitment, performance reviews should focus on goals, productivity, and quality of work.

Employers should endorse and help create legitimate, nontraditional career paths. Part-time standards must apply to both men and women. The success of part-time arrangements should not hinge on the goodwill of a supervisor. Fair guidelines up front can prevent both employer and employee from feeling that each is being taken advantage by the other. It is reasonable to expect a part-timer to give up some of the perks, but there is no reason for her to give up her career entirely.

What are the incentives for employers to offer family-friendly practices?

Women will soon constitute 50 percent of the work force. By tackling head-on the problems created by the glass ceiling and the maternal wall, employers will be able to retain the services of the best and brightest of their female professionals, making their companies more competitive in the marketplace. Family-friendly practices will also foster recruitment, retention, loyalty, good morale, reduced absenteeism, and high productivity among employees at all levels of the work force. Employees cannot be at their best if they come to work burdened by worries about the care of their children. To accomplish these changes, however, will require courage and determination by employers to do what has never been done before: to achieve full equality between men and women in the workplace.

What will these policies accomplish?

They may not work miracles—at least not right away. No level of family benefits can make all trade-offs between careers and children disappear. *But*, the potential for collision between the two can be reduced dramatically, with exciting results for both employer and employee.

Following are examples of what organizations can do to lessen some of the inevitable conflicts between profession and family:

The Basics: Child and Elder Care

- Resource and referral for child- and elder-care options.

- On-site day-care centers.

- Consortium arrangements to pool resources and support a day-care center between area businesses or between local day-care centers and public school systems.

- A cafeteria of benefits for child care and elder care: flexible (tax-advantage) benefit programs for dependent care and medical expense.

- Support for the after-school care of children.

- School vacation programs to provide coverage while parents work when schools are closed.

- Emergency and backup child care, either in facilities or with subsidies.

- Sick-child care: allow parents to use their own sick days, subsidize paid in-home care, or provide a sick-child center.

The Creative: A New Way to Work

- Use of vacation time in part-day increments: for doctor's appointments, school plays, and family emergencies.

- Flextime at all levels of an organization: core business hours established for all employees.

- Compressed workweeks: for example, four 9- or 10-hour days.

- Job sharing for both support staff and managers.

- Part-time work.

- Parental leave that is genuinely supported and encouraged for both men and women.

- Phased work reentry after parental leave: for example, half-time for several months before returning to a full-time schedule.

- Telecommuting and working from the home: depending upon the nature of the work, can be a short-term option or a long-term arrangement.

- Lunchtime seminars to share and address concerns of working parents (e.g., how to select quality child care, how to plan for a maternity leave, strategies for managing alternative work options).

- Periodic employee focus groups to determine the most pressing dependent-care concerns and to incorporate recommendations into institutional planning.

- Regular family-friendly audits to gauge an organization's success in promoting and retaining women, and to track the extent to which women and men use parental benefits.

The Secret to Success

Attitudinal support represents the real secret to success in recruiting and retaining talented employees who also happen to be parents. While support from the top is critical, it is not enough. Senior, midlevel, and line managers play a crucial role in how well the policies on the books are put into operation. Various techniques can be used to involve management personnel:

- Offer training programs for managers and supervisors on issues related to the work/family balance: subjects can include how to supervise and evaluate part-timers and job-share teams, and how to provide coverage for parental leaves.

- Require gender-awareness training to address workplace sexism that can hinder a woman's career advancement or cause her to seek another job.

- Develop new standards for performance reviews based on clear outcome measures and productivity rather than on less objective standards such as face time.

Finally, a piece of advice for the wise employee: Do what's right for you. Consider the quality of your life. Rely on priorities that work for you.

A California MBA said it well. "Each woman must make the decision that is right for her. But I think most women will be surprised at how much their lives change after they have children and at the depth of their feelings. When you wake up at 40, I think that your personal life becomes more important. Will your company remember you when you're 65?"

CHAPTER NINE

◆ ◆ ◆

Voices of the New Revolution

Every working mother seeks a solution to her individual dilemma of how to balance and reconcile her competing roles. The experiences of 902 of the most talented women in the country reveal a stark and, at first, discouraging reality. This group of lawyers, physicians, and MBAs tell us that exceptional education and top-notch professional training are not enough to eliminate the barriers imposed by the maternal wall. Even women who do not miss a professional beat once they become mothers risk unfair judgments and penalties imposed by bosses and co-workers. Solely because of the difference in one chromosome, today's professional women are forced to make a painful choice between careers and children.

It is the rare individual who can run an international conglomerate and find time to make cookies for the PTA. Yet there is no logical or business rationale for perpetuating the old rules of work that virtually ignore the realities of daily life for dual-career couples and single parents.

This unyielding corporate mentality places unnecessary stress on working mothers, no matter what their job level; on their families; and, consequently, on the workplace itself. Parents worry about the stressful model of work/family conflict that they are passing on to their own children.

When they can, today's women are finding new ways to achieve the best of both worlds: striking out on their own, or leaving one employer for another more friendly to families. Some women leave the work force entirely because they cannot negotiate an alternative work schedule or a part-time position. For many working mothers, economic realities limit the range of options available to them. These women and their families continue to absorb all the inherent stress between work and family.

THE NEED FOR A COLLECTIVE VOICE

Although the eloquent and often poignant voices of the trailblazing women we met seemed muted by frustration, fatigue, and guilt, we also detected a sense of hope, determination, and expectation that there can be real change in America's workplace. A persuasive, dynamic collective voice is needed if working mothers are to effect this profound change. If they succeed, they will enhance and even revolutionize the rules of work for men and women. And for their children, they will have forged new models for achieving the best from both career and family.

A Three-Step Plan

The stories of 902 women convinced us that the first step in this revolution must be a complete overhaul of the mores and rules of the workplace. The second phase must involve changing the attitudes and perceptions that have for too long fortified and protected these ancient traditions of the professions. The third step must focus on changes outside the office, in the form of increased support from spouses, families, and legislation.

Another critical step in the success of the new revolution for working parents will be the passage of legislation to ensure certain basic rights for all parents. When necessary, litigation must be used to enforce these laws. The success of this revolutionary process will be judged by the scope of life choices available, without penalty, to parents—women and men—who want and need to work without missing out on a meaningful life outside the office.

The first phase of the feminist movement focused on achieving the same opportunities for women to use their talents and pursue their careers that men had. And women have, in fact, gained entry into traditionally male-dominated professions. But true equality in the workplace still remains a distant reality.

Today's postfeminist woman grew up expecting a whole range of opportunities that had been denied to her mother's generation. Some took for granted the achievements of the generations of women preceding them. Not forced to fight the same types of battle—entry into professional schools and traditional male jobs—they thought the war was over. They were wrong. Postfeminists now face a struggle far more subtle and, perhaps, more difficult. Discrimination against the advancement of women in the workplace because of gender (the glass ceiling) or because of the decision to become a mother (the maternal wall) has taken a less visible course; but it is, as the individual voices in this book tell us, more insidious and more immune from recourse.

Solutions to the work/family dilemma cannot be achieved in the absence of solid acceptance and ongoing support from all levels of management. Mandated change is not a solution in and of itself. Family-friendly work rules, whether manifested in state parental leave laws or in company personnel policies, can be undermined through loopholes and inequities. Putting generous parental leave benefits on the books is not enough if, off the record and behind the scenes, employees are discouraged from taking advantage of these policies by those responsible for their day-to-day implementation.

The New Demographics

Sixty-seven percent of U.S. mothers with children aged 18 or younger now work outside the home.[1] In this group are a growing number of single parents who do not have the option of support at home. Discrimination against working women is bad for business, if not evident in the short-term, certainly over the long-run. "The Census Bureau reports that the number of women entering the labor force with a college degree is rising 1.5 times as fast as the number of men. . ."[2]

An alarming number of the 902 women we surveyed told us they are exiting from the traditional work culture because it is, all too often, blatantly hostile to them. This loss of trained and qualified workers will be all the more troubling by the year 2000, when 47 percent of the employed population is projected to be women.[3] At a time when America's worldwide competitiveness is under intense attack, it is both shortsighted and counter-productive for corporate America to force talented women to leave their employ and seek less demanding employment else-where because of a failure to recognize basic family needs.

Old attitudes die hard. The traditions of an unyielding work culture are so firmly in place and so rarely questioned that women have become accustomed to managing intense conflict between profession and family, with all of the accommodation between the two falling on the family. Many women justifiably fear the economic repercussions of rocking the boat. Others, even if perilously close to personal burnout, worry about being perceived only as "whiners" who are lucky enough to hold good jobs.

Believing that they are somehow the source of the problem, working mothers too often feel forced to choose between two extremes. They can either drop out and lower self-esteem and family income or remain stoic while leading overburdened and highly stressed lives. Unfortunately, maintaining their silence perpetuates the work-must-always-supersede-family mentality and leaves the maternal wall intact. Yet when these women drop off the fast track, no one understands why.

When genuine support is fragile, the work/family merger is tenuous and stressful for both parents and children. When management refuses to recognize and support the realities of the family social structure outside the office, the probability of collision between dedication to career and commitment to family is enormously high. The penalty for employers who fail to provide this support is corporate brain drain and the loss of talent important to their bottom line.

Too many of those at the top of their organizations have been reluctant to relinquish the Ozzie and Harriet myth as the standard for life outside the office. The overwhelming majority of employers have only just begun to respond to the demographic profile of today's work force. Thus, the standard work ethic continues to be predicated on the assumption that there is a woman at home full-time to manage family life. This faulty assumption perpetuates and intensifies the work/family dilemma faced by women and their families.

DISILLUSIONMENT: A SPRINGBOARD FOR CHANGE

In "The Mixed Legacy of Women's Liberation," Alvin Sanoff finds some reason for optimism in the predicament of today's working mother. He notes that "a look at women's history suggests that such periods of disillusionment often contain the seeds for the next stage of social change."[4] Unless women, and men as well, begin to exert pressure on their employers, however, nothing will shake the sturdy foundation of the maternal wall. Women are beginning to take action on their disillusionment, primarily by changing jobs or becoming their own bosses. While these actions help women to reconcile their own work/family dilemma, ironically they let employers off the hook for the short-run by not forcing them to confront the problem.

Charting new territory in a work culture that begrudges change and still calls upon women to prove themselves, simply because they are women, will not be accomplished without encountering roadblocks. If we women are to move ahead and make lasting progress for our children's generation, we must put aside judgments, particularly among ourselves, of what constitutes a "good" mother or a "committed" worker.

Many women still feel compelled to downplay their "other life," and with good reason. They have witnessed firsthand instances where a woman is penalized for being "too much of a mother" because she leaves the office in time for dinner. At the other extreme, a woman risks being categorized by neighbors or even family members as "just one of those tough career women" if she, by choice, returns to work full-time soon after a child is born.

Laura Tosi, Barbara Pearce, and Janet Shur each, against the backdrop of expectations held by past generations, experienced her own version of the need to prove herself in her new role. Laura had to prove to her father, her teachers and, finally, to herself that gender was no reason to forgo her clear ambition to enter one of the most demanding of professions, orthopedic surgery.

Barbara Pearce's well-intentioned and supportive father had difficulty accepting that his daughter's maternal instincts would not diminish her business acumen. Janet Shur had to put aside the new role expectations for her generation before she could feel comfortable with carrying more of the child-care responsibility, making much less money than her husband, and starting a nontraditional part-time law practice.

Alice Rogoff, with a little help from technology, decided to defy the odds against being a part-time chief financial officer. For the immediate future, Audrey Kadis has found her calling as a social action fund-raiser. Pat Jacobs thrives on having too much on her plate—three children, single parenthood, her own booming business—because she does it on her own terms and according to her own rules of work.

It all comes down to quality of life. Convinced that there must be a better way to be both a parent and a professional, these women refused to listen to the voices that dictated how professionals with their credentials should be leading their lives. Each woman decided what was best for her and her family, a decision that should come without a stigma automatically being attached.

The Payoff for Families

The concept of superwoman may be dying, but women continue to "do" it all. Women who work full-time in the office still manage a second shift in the home. Small wonder that women in the 1990s have applied so little overt pressure to effect change in their work environment. They have no time or energy left at the end of the day to deal with any issues. But such inaction is shortsighted. With the tone of a grandfather whose own daughters work outside the home, pediatrician T. Berry Brazelton reminds us that there are human payoffs for investing in the needs of parents and their children of the next generation:

> *"Improving conditions for working parents has a visible payoff. When parents have options and can make their own choices, they feel respected and secure. Men walk differently as they enter my office. A father who is participating actively in his child's care walks straighter, has a more jaunty air, and he can't wait to tell me about each of his baby's successes. A working mother who has found a balance between her work and her family speaks more decisively. She handles her baby with assurance and is eager to include her solutions in our discussion of her child's progress. These parents are empowered. Helping others to feel the way they do is an investment in the future."[5]*

The Costs for Business

For businesses, it's a question of judgment and taking a longer-term perspective on benefits and employee retention. Not only

223

does the unnecessary collision between careers and children take a personal toll on family life, it also affects productivity by alienating people from their companies and their professions. By making it difficult for half of the work population to use their skills and talents fully, business is penalizing itself and jeopardizing its future growth. Corporate America itself must face head-on the reality of corporate brain drain and deal effectively and forcefully with the impact of this self-imposed penalty.

The gap that persists between policy and practice of family benefits must be narrowed. Ellen Galinsky, co-president of the Families and Work Institute in New York, discovered that in one U.S. company known for its progressive family benefits "52 percent of the employees reported that they believed taking advantage of the company's time and leave programs would jeopardize their jobs or careers."[6]

Parents—women *and* men—should not be punished for their desire to invest time and energy in the next generation. Parental benefits should not be labeled as offers of "special treatment" for women. A growing number of fathers who are dedicated to their careers and have wives in the work force are determined to lead their lives according to a set of standards different from those of their own fathers'. Parental leave is not a selfish demand. It is good business.

WOMEN'S QUEST FOR BALANCED LIVES

The women we met have set out to achieve balance, as opposed to burnout, in fulfilling their professional ambitions while finding time to enjoy their families. They refuse to believe that these are mutually exclusive goals. Putting family first need not derail career success and reward. Certain trade-offs are inevitable for anyone juggling multiple roles, but success in one role can enhance the energy and commitment to another. This important message has not yet permeated corporate culture.

A large percentage of the women we surveyed were surprised by the strength of the maternal pull and were at first discouraged by the unnecessary obstacles in the workplace to merging two important aspects of their identities. As they began to experience the barriers that have traditionally perpetuated the separation of maternal and professional identities, they developed a fierce determination to seek their own unique solutions to the work/family dilemma. In so doing, they have begun to dismantle the traditional expectations that have fortified the maternal wall. By casting aside preconceptions and misconceptions about how to be both a parent and a professional, they have become the pioneers for new models of balance between work and family.

An emerging respect for the time, energy, and stamina required to be a parent supports today's quest for balance between career and children. Many women readily acknowledged that they find parenthood infinitely more challenging than any of their professional responsibilities. There is nothing wrong in admitting to the joys of motherhood. Neither should there be a stigma attached to fulfilling professional ambition.

An evolving and visible quest for more quality leisure and personal time, along with an acknowledgment of the demands on today's employee from both children and elder parents, has heightened the need for radical change in the quest for balance. Today's woman is rewriting her roles for the 1990s and the next century within a complicated and often conflicting context: the history and experience of past generations of family; her own self-imposed expectations; the structure and demands of her professional life; and the norms of our work culture and our social culture.

The media's portrayal of the work/family dilemma reflects the divergent and extraordinarily complicated social questions raised by the emergence of new roles for both women and men. For instance, a 1992 advertisement for IBM pictures a father and young daughter leaning over a home computer. The ad copy explains how this company's product can assist the often delicate work/family balance:

> "The first computer to understand you don't just have a job. You have a life. Something fundamental has changed in America. Now it's not just the living you make, it's the life you make. You want to enjoy the things you're supposedly working for. Your family. Your home. Yourself."[7]

At the other end of the spectrum, showing how low expectations can be for the evolution of women's roles, a follow-up editorial to a 1992 *Fortune* cover story on corporate women lapsed into the traditional corporate sports metaphors, advising women that "to play the game, we have to step up to the plate."[8] Even worse, the editorial implies that women are the ultimate source of discrimination in the workplace and advises them to "lighten up a little" and behave more like the men. "Stepping up to the plate means joining management clubs, accepting job transfers, pushing for line jobs and fair compensation, working on deficiencies, and cultivating relationships. . ."[9]

The problem with this advice is that it ignores the reality that many women and men do not want to live by the old rules of the game that insist that ambition and commitment to a career preclude being able to enjoy a family life.

A *New York Times* article entitled "Women at the Top: Role Models or Relics?" questions whether recent college graduates want to follow the patterns set by executive women who have copied the lives of traditional executive males. A conference panelist addressing the topic observed that women beginning their careers today "want a more balanced life-style early on. . . . While the [executive] women achieved very senior levels before demanding life-style changes, the new work force wants them early. It's not that the fire in the belly is missing now, but it's been tempered."[10] We would suggest that the fire in the belly really has not been tempered, but it has spread in two conflicting directions.

A 1991 *Working Woman* management column on alternative work options featured this gloomy response from a male CEO on flextime: "I have a hard time with flextime. It's not that I don't trust employees, but a disciplined work environment is heavily influenced by peer pressure."[11] While this perspective on the culture of work probably reflects the prevailing attitude among senior executives, companies that have experimented with alternative work options have found them workable and a force in the retention of valued employees. Leadership is the resource that holds the clout to change the workplace rules.

And what can we expect in the way of change in the home? A recent study of MBA students at the Wharton School was not encouraging. The study found that "compared with their female classmates, men gave a lower priority to spending 'quality time' with their spouses, sharing housework and child care and minimizing excess travel on the job."[12] Yet, the women we interviewed who were the most satisfied with their work/family balance credited their husbands with playing a key role in co-parenting and in supporting their careers.

Although Gerald Holton, a Harvard professor of physics, has specifically investigated the barriers to the progress of women in science, his findings are broadly applicable to other mothers in the work force. He refers to one of the obstacles to career progress as the synchronizing of three clocks: "their biological clock, their career clock, and their spouse's career clock."[13] As a result of a survey of women scientists, Professor Holton concludes:

> *"The young woman scientist has to deal with a much larger and more complex universe than her academically equivalent male. The kind of institutions we have set up, including promotions, the lack of part-time employment, the lack of*

childcare in many places . . . are all weighing very heavily on women who have to manage those three different clocks.''[14]

Taking a broad and long-term perspective on life and career clocks can help both employer and employee forge new models for career development and professional progression. Few people can simultaneously focus on professional status and adequate family time without some trade-offs, yet most people want and need to maintain an ongoing commitment to both, without long-term sacrifice of either.

A CALL TO ACTION

If every mother or woman contemplating motherhood, whether a secretary or the president of a company, refused to work at organizations not friendly to families, business in the country would come to a screeching halt. Disturbing and far-fetched as this fantasy may be, it points to the potential power held by working women unified to lobby for benefits, policies, and practices that realistically recognize the responsibilities faced by all parents.

The fundamental goals of this generation of working women are:

1. To provide family income and to use their talents and abilities in meaningful work in their professions.

2. To enjoy the rewards and satisfactions of a rich and rewarding family life.

For women who want both, the playing field can be leveled only by a radical transformation in the structure of work. Dismantling the maternal wall will force more cracks in the glass ceiling. Men who want to be involved fathers will also benefit from a reconfigured work culture more accepting of a host of new options for meeting the requirements of a job.

In the stories of our respondents, we heard the voice of a

generation of women who at times appeared almost desperate to resolve the work/family dilemma in a fair and equitable way—for both employer and employee: Neither employer nor employee should perceive that they are being taken advantage of by the other. Nor should the basic demands of career or the fundamental needs of family be forced onto a collision course, as has happened to this generation of professional women. They should not have to pursue one at the expense of the other. The economic realities of dual-career couples and single parents dictate the necessity for most people to work outside the home. This is more than just a "woman's problem."

Women and men who want better balance in their lives need to make their collective voices heard. This is a call to action for parents. The number of dual-career couples rose from 52 percent in 1980 to 63 percent in 1988, while the number of single-parent households rose by 23 percent in that decade.[15] Given these numbers, it is not unrealistic to speculate about the potential power that can be wielded by a critical segment of the working population. A call to action does not suggest that any woman should risk losing her livelihood. Not everyone has the luxury of picking and choosing from job offers.

What Employees Can Do

What kind of power can women realistically exert? How can they seize control of their right to choose how they lead their lives? What kind of influence do women really hold over their work environment? They can refuse a job. They can leave one job and take another. They can join forces within their work environment to effect change. They can use their clout when they get to the top. Collective action provides strength and support. Voting with your feet gets notice and results.

The revelation that "OK, at least I know it's not me" is the foundation for beginning to fight back against rules of the workplace that make little sense for a growing and important segment of the labor pool. Persistent patterns of behavior in the work culture that pit careers against family are usually unwritten and often unspoken, yet they are deeply ingrained in the basic fabric of the culture.

At first glance, a poor economy and America's serious failings in international business competition may seem to justify postponing the introduction of untried concepts into the culture of work. But employers really have no choice in the matter. In fact, an overhaul of the rules of work could open up exciting possibilities for new standards of employee productivity and more accurate measures of employee performance.

What needs to happen now is to reignite the collective anger and frustration demonstrated in the earlier phases of the feminist movement. Anger and frustration can incite movement toward change. These seemingly negative emotions have been the positive catalyst for many successful self-employment ventures and fueled confidence in the entrepreneurs we met. These women are spearheading an important trend. The National Foundation for Women Business Owners projects that women-owned companies are now on the verge of surpassing Fortune 500 companies in the number of new job openings.[16]

Clout means influence. Clout will come when women act collectively—in their unions, through informal and formal networking, and by joining with male colleagues who share goals for a reasonable work/family balance. Midlevel managers not yet senior enough to initiate change from above can lobby for task forces and work-climate assessments to gather information about real (and often unspoken) employee needs. Senior level executives can foster and, in fact, require a major overhaul in policies and attitudes on the needs of families. They can mandate training programs for managers and institute family-friendly work-climate audits for their organizations.

Lobbying for federal legislation to support family needs and protect the rights of working parents is yet another forum for collective action. With the increased number of women in Congress and at all levels of government, the stage has been set for legislation to support social change that is long overdue.

Women who have risen to positions of power have an obligation to redefine and humanize a workplace that has ignored the radical and irreversible changes taking place on the home front. Women at the top and in the middle of their organizations need to serve as career mentors to younger women. Mentoring is another tactic for accelerating the change to a more realistic work/family merger. Effective mentoring provides one more opportunity to broaden the range of career choices offered to the new breed of parent/professional. Mentors can begin to dispel some of the myths about part-time careers, about the validity of face time, and about gender as an inherent penalty.

What Employers Can Do

Employers working to foster change can promote small victories by showing how effective and profitable alternative work options can be. All it takes is one or two examples of successful part-timers or job-sharing teams to break down the fear that flextime equals chaos.

Supervisors at all levels of the work force play a critical role in the policy-versus-practice conundrum. Without question, backing from the top is crucial to assure that new and different work rules will succeed in practice.

Backing from the top is not enough, however. The best intentions of upper management can fall flat without the support of front-line supervisors who can, and do, determine the critical workplace climate. Senior managers and line supervisors can encourage employees to use benefits that make it easier to be committed to a job without sacrificing family. Some progressive companies are demonstrating their commitment to both public schools and to parenting by allowing employees two hours a month of paid time to volunteer in the local schools.

Although only 15 percent of U.S. companies offer unpaid leave for employees to care for sick family members,[17] many corporations have begun to see positive bottom-line results from their family-friendly policies:

• • •

Since Aetna Life and Casualty began offering flexible work options and six months' unpaid parental leave, "the company cut its post-maternity attrition rate from 24 percent to 12 percent."[18]

• • •

A study by the Catalyst research firm of 50 companies that provide alternative work options revealed that these benefits enhanced employee retention, recruitment, productivity, and morale. "Almost two-thirds (65 percent) reported that employees who utilize flexible work arrangements sustained higher productivity."[19]

• • •

The Families and Work Institute reported the financial trade-offs between leave policies and employee replacement costs: "A study of one company with a one-year family leave policy found it was three to five times more expensive to replace the employee than to hold the job open for the employee's return."[20]

• • •

The SAS Institute, a software developer with an on-site child-care center, has a "low 7 percent turnover rate, compared with the nationwide average of 25 percent in the computer industry."[21]

• • •

Family-friendly policies at Corning, including part-time work and job sharing, reduced employee turnover by 50 percent,[22] cutting attrition costs by $2 million a year.[23]

• • •

Is it worth it for an employer to invest in someone who might temporarily drop out of the work force? The answer is yes. The statistics are definitely in the employer's favor. In addition, there is no guarantee of employee loyalty and retention under any circumstances. Men and women leave jobs for a whole host of acceptable reasons, but it is bad corporate policy to fail, by perpetuating outdated policies and work rules, a significant number of employees who might otherwise stay.

We met many talented women with families whose first alternative choice was for part-time employment rather than leaving the work force. Most professionals seek full-time work, with the right to take a maternity leave without penalty and with provision for some occasional flexibility. If policies are fair and positive attitudes underlie them, women will return to work after their maternity leaves with high morale and solid productivity.

There is no logical reason why a reasonable maternity leave should be detrimental to either a woman's career or her employer. With advance planning, fortified by clear and honest communication between employer and employee, a parental leave is a benefit that can work with minimal pain to the organization. Parents should not be forced to deny—because of fear of job loss, demotion, or loss of respect—their desire to spend time with a newborn.

If a woman's pregnancy allows her to work full pace up until delivery (and this is the case for most women), is there any good reason why ongoing clients and projects should be reassigned during her pregnancy without other cause? When a woman returns from a maternity leave, she can hit the ground running if her job is really held for her and if peers and bosses do not treat her differently or shut her off from her responsibilities.

Part-time and flexible work options represent untapped reservoirs of employee potential and should be accorded respect and support as legitimate and productive career options. The loudest call to employers, however, should be for flexibility. Many people cannot afford to reduce their hours. Some can afford to work part-time only for a few years. Flexibility, which is essential to involved parenting, can be as simple as arranging schedules so that one spouse works from 7:00 A.M. to 3:00 P.M. and the other, from 9:00 A.M. to 6:00 P.M.

Working at home and telecommuting from home, even if only on an occasional basis, can help solve the logistical nightmare of how to care for a sick child or how to attend a school event in the middle of the day. Phased return from maternity leave, with an initial part-time schedule, can address problems of coverage for the employer as well as extend partial leave for the employee. Allowing employees to extend lunch hours or use hourly increments of their vacation time to attend school events or a doctor's appointment can alleviate the kind of stress that lowers both productivity and morale.

Part-time work should not automatically place a career on hold; however, subtle attitudes and hostile day-to-day behavior from bosses and co-workers can jeopardize the chances of success for this alternative work option. The part-timer who leaves at 4:00 P.M. is more often than not subjected to not-so-discreet glances at the watch by co-workers who refuse to accept part-time work as a legitimate career option and who forget that the part-timer is paid less than they are.

While these recommendations for new rules of work are not on the surface profound changes, they are simple, straightforward, and practical measures that will go far to minimize the impact of parenting on working women and their employers.

DISMANTLING THE MATERNAL WALL

Taught by a recession that job security can be short lived, and observant that many current leaders missed too much of their own children's growing up, today's women are determined to avoid the potentially restrictive trappings of traditional success. Many are beginning to scale down their life-style expectations. While not everyone reaches a standard of living that permits scaling down, the strategy of reducing economic vulnerability can provide choices and options, particularly for women and men who want to work part-time.

What steps can a woman take to reduce the potential for collision between work and family? Here are some suggestions:

- Evaluate your work environment at the onset of your employment (and throughout your tenure), and do everything possible to be in a family-friendly organization when your children are born. Reduce the likelihood of hitting the maternal wall by assessing—as a matter of principle—the commitment of even your first employer to the needs of family. Although you may not yet have children or plans to stay with the organization for the long term, this effort will arm you with information about how to read the family-friendly index in future work settings.

- If possible, establish yourself professionally before having children. This can be helpful on two counts: first, you may be in a better position to negotiate the length of your maternity leave and any flexibility that you require in a work schedule; second, you will have a clearer sense of your own priorities and of how you want to balance your life.

- Negotiate with your spouse as to how you will share parental and household responsibilities. Talk about the division of parental duties before you marry. Try to plan for the future, recognizing that your own upbringing has influenced the expectations you hold for each of your own roles. Be honest with one another and realistic about the demands required by each of your careers and how they will affect family responsibilities. Continue to update these agreements with your spouse as circumstances change at work or at home. Fairness and comfort with choices is infinitely more important than absolute parity in every role.

- Negotiate with your employer from a position of strength. If you have already established a solid and visible track record in your job, you will have a better chance at securing a flexible schedule or reduced hours. If you propose an alternative work option that has not previously been tried, suggest a review period to assess the impact of the arrangement on clients and on job productivity.

- Assert your influence on parenting policies whenever you can. If you leave a job and are securely out the door with good references and a new job, volunteer for an exit interview. Address any stated policies as well as negative attitudes toward working mothers that result from the subtle and dangerous barriers imposed by the less-visible side of the maternal wall.

- Keep the logistics as simple as possible. Avoid long commutes for either work or child care. Arrange backup child care. Plan in advance with your spouse how you will cover sick-child days and school vacations.

- Even during years of high earnings be fiscally conservative, recognizing that one parent may want to reduce hours in the future to accommodate the needs of your young children.

- Recognize that few decisions are risk free. Allow some provision for failure, for regrouping. Take individual stock periodically at your own personal, private annual meeting. Ask yourself: Am I leading my life the way *I* want to? Is my work environment supportive of working mothers? If not, can I change it? Is it time to bail out and switch gears in my career?

- Give yourself the option of changing your life-style as family responsibilities change and as career priorities evolve.

- Rely on your own standards for personal "success." Do not be afraid to challenge conventional notions of what constitutes commitment to a profession. Be daring about new ideas for work/family balance and undaunted by corporate myopia.

- Refuse to apologize for your choices. Define your own unique roles that work for you and your family and tune out expectations from those who have made a different set of choices. Don't let others dictate how you lead your life. Your confidence and your persistence are bound to influence how you are perceived and treated in the workplace.

As women begin to make their individual decisions in the work/family merger, a new pattern is emerging. It is a pattern that emphasizes choice over tradition to ensure a balanced life in which one can be an "involved" mother and a "committed" professional at the same time.

Women have discovered, on their own, new strategies to

manage the work/family merger. They have begun to go public with their personal dilemma without apology for wanting more family time, recognizing that there is no one right way to lead a balanced life. Women *will* have it all, within the context of new rules in the office and new expectations in the home, and on terms best for them, their families, and their employers. And women will create a new definition of success, one that allows them to satisfy and enjoy both of their critical commitments: to work and to home.

SURVEY BACKGROUND

The statistical analysis of 902 returned surveys out of the 1,644 mailed became the basis for this book. The fact that so many extraordinarily busy women chose to respond to a detailed six-page questionnaire confirmed our assumption that the quest to achieve balance in the work/family dilemma is an issue critically important for women today. We deliberately selected a group of women who, we believed, would already have had important personal experience with the challenges of achieving balance between their careers and their children.

Based on the patterns that emerged from the written surveys, we chose to interview 52 women whose life choices and experiences were representative of the larger sample of mothers. The statistics came alive through the honest, and at times shocking, stories from mothers in the professions of business, law, and medicine.

Our survey was designed to elicit responses from both parents and non-parents on how they have reached decisions in their work/family choices. For example, 85 percent of the 902 women believe that reducing hours of work is detrimental to a woman's career. Despite this widely held perception, 70 percent of the women with children decreased their hours after the birth of their first child. Knowing that the traditional rules of a male-dominated work culture challenge their role as a parent, the Harvard women demonstrated a fierce determination to forge new definitions for being an involved parent *and* a committed professional.

In answer to our last survey question "Have you been able to combine career and family successfully?", 85 percent of the mothers responded "yes," although many qualified their responses with comments such as: "Ask me again in ten years" or "It depends on what day of the week you ask me." The less than rousing "yeses" reflect the complexity of women's multiple roles and reveal their personal efforts to balance on a daily basis the two important aspects of their lives: profession and family.

Survey Results

Who Responded

From the Classes of 1971 to 1981	Number of Surveys Mailed Summer 1990	Number of Surveys Returned	Response Rate (%)
Harvard Business School (HBS)	586	341	58
Harvard Law School (HLS)	668	332	50
Harvard Medical School (HMS)	390	229	59
TOTAL	1,644	902	55

Profile of the 902 Women
66 Percent Are Mothers

Age Groups		Marital Status	
32–39	58%	Single	16%
40–49	40%	Married	76%
50–57	2%	Divorced	7%
		Separated	1%
		Widowed	—*

Number of Children		Ages of Children		Age of Woman When First Child Was Born	
1	28%	5 or younger	53%	Under 30	21%
2	52%	6–18	41%	30–39	76%
3	16%	18+	6%	40+	3%
4–7	4%				

Employment Status

	Employed (%)	Not Employed (%)	Why They Changed Jobs**
All Respondents			58% of all respondents changed
HBS	81	19	jobs in the last 5 years for the
HLS	91	9	following reasons:
HMS	96	4	Professional development 71%
Mothers in Survey			Family responsibilities 38%
HBS	75	25	Financial reasons 19%
HLS	89	11	
HMS	96	4	

Opinions on Actions Detrimental to a Woman's Career	Yes (%)	No (%)
Taking a maternity leave of 6 weeks or less	12	88
Reduce hours of work	85	15
Refuse to work evenings or weekends	91	9
Refuse to travel	90	10
Miss work due to child's illness	55	45

Advice for Other Women Confronting the Work/Family Dilemma
(Open-ended response)

Set priorities	28%
Don't sacrifice your personal life	19%
Make compromises	17%
Don't postpone family life	5%
Have confidence in your decisions	3%
Keep work and family separate	3%
Choose employer carefully	3%

Profile of the 594 Mothers
Length of Maternity Leave

Number of Months	First Child (%)	Second Child (%)
0	2	7
1	10	10
2	28	27
3	25	24
4	17	13
5	3	5
6	9	8
7–12	6	6

*Type of Child Care Used***

Daily help in home	58%
Live-in help	42%
Day care center	33%
Family day care	25%

How First Child Affected Hours Worked

Decreased hours	70%
Maintained hours	28%
Increased hours	2%

How Parenting Affected Careers

	Yes (%)	No (%)
Changed job responsibilities or specialty	53	47
Refused job or promotion	30	70
Lost out on job or promotion	18	82

*Tradeoffs Made in the Work/Family Merger***

Slowed career advancement	39%
Not enough time for children	25%
No time for self	25%
No time for husband	11%
Earn less money	11%
Fatigue	9%
No time for friends	8%
No hobbies	7%

Have you been successful at combining career and family?

Yes	85%
No	12%
Undecided	3%

* —Less than .5%
**—Multiple responses checked
Percentages are based on those who answered each question.

NOTES

◆ ◆ ◆

INTRODUCTION

1. Feminist Majority Foundation, "Empowering Women in Business," 1990, 11.

2. Nina Darton, "Mommy vs. Mommy," *Newsweek*, 4 June 1990, 66.

3. Dana E. Friedman and Ellen Galinsky, "Work and Family Trends," Families and Work Institute, 1991, 2.

4. "The Great Experiment," *Time*, Special Issue, "Women: The Road Ahead," Fall 1990, 72.

5. Shirley Chisholm, *The Good Fight* (New York: Harper & Row, 1973).

6. Betty Friedan, *The Feminine Mystique* (New York: Dell, 1963), 15.

CHAPTER ONE

1. Judith Mandelbaum-Schmid, "An Unequal Past, A Common Future," *MD*, May 1992, 88.

2. Sharyn Lenhart, "What Does It Mean to Be Pregnant at

Harvard?" Conference proceedings, *Parenting and Working in the Harvard Medical Community: Is the Price Too High?* Joint Committee on the Status of Women, 1987, 17.

3. Ibid., 19–20.

4. Ibid., 19.

5. Wendy Kaminer, *A Fearful Freedom* (Reading, Mass.: Addison-Wesley Publishing Co., 1990), 93.

6. Diane Harris, "You're Pregnant? You're Out," *Working Woman*, August 1992, 50.

7. Kaminer, *A Fearful Freedom*, 36.

8. Harris, "You're Pregnant? You're Out," 51.

9. Ibid., 48.

10. Mark A. Klebanoff, et al., "Outcomes of Pregnancy in a National Sample of Resident Physicians," *The New England Journal of Medicine*, 323 (Oct. 11, 1990): 1040–1045.

11. "Study: Child's Diet Not Compromised by Career Mother." *The Boston Globe*, 5 Aug. 1992, 72.

12. T. Berry Brazelton, *Working and Caring* (Reading, Mass.: Addison-Wesley Publishing Co., 1985), 114.

CHAPTER TWO

1. Susan Estrich, "Reproductive Freedom," *Radcliffe Quarterly*, September 1989, 8.

2. Arlie Hochschild, *The Second Shift* (New York: Viking, 1989).

3. Mary Ann Mason, "The Equality Trap," *Working Mother*, September 1988, 38.

4. Story C. Landis, "Test Tubes and Babies," *Harvard Medical Alumni Bulletin*, Summer 1985, 30.

5. Claudia Wallis, "Onward, Women!" *Time*, 4 Dec. 1989, 86.

6. T. Berry Brazelton, Talk to the Joint Committee on the Status of Women and the Harvard Medical Center Office for Parenting, December 1989, 5.

7. T. Berry Brazelton, "Working Parents," *Newsweek*, 13 Feb. 1989, 67–70.

8. Carin Rubenstein, "Guilty or Not Guilty," *Working Mother*, May 1991, 56.

9. Sharyn Lenhart, "What Does It Mean to Be Pregnant at Harvard?" Conference proceedings, *Parenting and Working in the Harvard Medical Community: Is the Price Too High?* Joint Committee on the Status of Women, 1987, 17.

10. Donna K. Whitney, "A Physician's Perspective," *Emma Willard Bulletin*, Fall/Winter 1990, 10–11.

CHAPTER FOUR

1. Susan McHenry and Linda Lee Small, "Does Part-Time Pay Off?" *Ms.*, March 1989, 92.

2. "Work and Family Today: 100 Key Statistics," *The BNA Special Report Series on Work and Family*, special report no. 41, May 1991, 23.

3. Matina S. Horner, "Femininity and Successful Achievement: A Basic Inconsistency," in J. Bardwick et al., eds., *Feminine Personality and Conflict* (Belmont, Calif.: Brooks/Cole, 1970), 46.

4. Judith Mandelbaum-Schmid, "Are Some Doctors Less Equal Than Others?" *MD*, February 1992, 74.

5. Elizabeth Ehrlich, "The Mommy Track," *Business Week*, 20 Mar. 1989, 132.

6. Louise A. La Mothe, "Endangered Species," *Stanford Lawyer*, Spring/Summer 1989, 14.

CHAPTER FIVE

1. "Salary Survey 1993," *Working Woman*, January 1993, 43.

2. Nancy Roosa, "Sex, Savvy, and Money," *Boston Woman*, August 1988, 40.

3. Kenneth Labich, "The New Low-Risk Entrepreneurs," *Fortune*, 27 July 1992, 85.

4. "Women-Owned Businesses," *The Minuteman Chronicle*, 22 Aug. 1992, 1.

5. Labich, "The New Low-Risk Entrepreneurs," 84.

6. Ibid., 84.

CHAPTER SIX

1. Barbara Bush, "Cherish Your Human Connections," *Wellesley*, Summer 1990, 7, 43.

CHAPTER SEVEN

1. Carin Rubenstein, "The Joys of a 50/50 Marriage," *Working Mother*, April 1992, 60.

2. Barbara Goldberg, "Mr. Moms," *Middlesex News*, 16 June 1991, 1C, 3C.

3. Jill Smolowe, "When Jobs Clash," *Time*, 3 Sept. 1990, 82.

4. Brian O'Reilly, "Why Grade 'A' Execs Get an 'F' as Parents," *Fortune*, 1 Jan. 1990, 42–43.

5. Smolowe, "When Jobs Clash," 84.

CHAPTER EIGHT

1. Monci Jo Williams, "Women Beat the Corporate Game," *Fortune*, 12 Sept. 1988, 138.

2. Amanda Troy Segal, "Corporate Women," *Business Week*, 8 June 1992, 77.

3. Louise A. La Mothe, "Endangered Species," *Stanford Lawyer*, Spring/Summer 1989, 16.

4. Anne B. Fisher, "When Will Women Get to the Top?" *Fortune*, 21 Sept. 1992, 44.

5. Arlie Hochschild, *The Second Shift* (New York: Viking, 1989).

6. Walter Kiechel III, "Overscheduled, and Not Loving It," *Fortune*, 8 Apr. 1991, 105.

7. Juliet B. Schor, *The Overworked American* (New York: Basic Books, 1991), 161.

8. Douglas T. Hall and Judith Richter, "Balancing Work Life and Home Life: What Can Organizations Do to Help?" *Executive*, August 1988, 216.

9. Brian O'Reilly, "Why Grade 'A' Execs Get an 'F' as Parents," *Fortune*, 1 Jan. 1990, 42.

10. Diane Harris, "Maternity Leave Yours, Maternity Leave Hers," *Working Woman*, August 1991, 58.

11. "Work and Family Today: 100 Key Statistics," *The BNA Special Report Series on Work and Family*, special report no. 41, May 1991, 26.

12. "Parenting and the Legal Profession," *A Report of the Boston Bar Association Task Force on Parenting and the Legal Profession*, 1991, 5.

CHAPTER NINE

1. Sue Shellenbarger, "Women with Children Increase in Workforce," *The Wall Street Journal*, 12 Feb. 1992, section B, p. 1., col. 1.

2. "Salary Survey 1993," *Working Woman*, January 1993, 40.

3. "Flexible Work Arrangements: Establishing Options for Managers and Professionals," Executive Summary (New York: Catalyst, 1990), 1.

4. Alvin P. Sanoff, "The Mixed Legacy of Women's Liberation," *U.S. News & World Report*, 12 Feb. 1990, 61.

5. T. Berry Brazelton, "Working Parents," *Newsweek*, 13 Feb. 1989, 70.

6. Ellen Galinsky, "Work and Family: 1992," Status Report and Outlook (New York, New York: The Families and Work Institute, 1992), 3.

7. IBM advertisement, *Time*, 19 Oct. 1992, 15.

8. Nancy J. Perry, "If You Can't Join 'Em, Beat 'Em," *Fortune*, 21 Sept. 1992, 59.

9. Ibid.

10. Barbara Lyne, "Women at the Top: Role Models or Relics?" *The New York Times*, 27 Sept. 1992, F27.

11. Andrew S. Grove, "Does Out of Sight Mean Out of Mind?" *Working Woman*, December 1991, 19.

12. Gilbert Fuchsberg, "Change Is Slow in Views on Two-Career Couples," *The Wall Street Journal*, 24 Feb. 1991, B1.

13. "On the Need to Remove Barriers to Women in Science," *Harvard University Gazette*, 2 Oct. 1992, 6.

14. Ibid.

15. "Work and Family Today: 100 Key Statistics," *The BNA Special Report Series on Work and Family*, special report no. 41, May 1991, 25.

16. "Women-Owned Businesses," *The Minuteman Chronicle*, 22 Aug. 1992, 1.

17. "Businesses Told to Take a Stand for Family Leave Legislation," *The National Report on Work and Family* (Washington, D.C.: Buraff Publications, 18 Feb. 1992), 6.

18. "Flexibility: Compelling Strategies for a Competitive Workplace," in *New Ways to Work in Partnership with Du Pont* (Wilmington, Del.: E.I. DuPont de Nemours & Co., 1991), 8.

19. "Flexible Work Arrangements: Establishing Options for Managers and Professionals," Executive Summary, 1.

20. "Facts and Figures," *The National Report on Work and Family*, 12 May 1992, 5.

21. "Businesses Told to Take a Stand for Family Leave Legisla-

tion," *The National Report on Work and Family*, 18 Feb. 1992, 7.

22. Annetta Miller and Dody Tsiantar, "Mommy Tracks," *Newsweek*, 25 Nov. 1991, 49.

23. Ellen Graham, "Flexible Formulas," *The Wall Street Journal*, 4 June 1990, R34.

INDEX

◆ ◆ ◆

Note: An asterisk indicates the use of a pseudonym.